AN ARROW
IN THE HAND

A mother's guide to influencing their

children to bring about generational impact

TERRELL MURPHY

ISBN:1718624409

CONTENTS

DEDICATION

This book is dedicated to my 82-year-old mother, Emma Louise Dula Murphy. Growing up I never realized the value of her as a mother to me and my brother Skip (about whom she always said, "I didn't name anything 'Skip.' That boy is named Tommy"). However, there are a few things that I am especially aware of: She always believed in me. She never gave up on me, and she was a firm believer that I could do anything that I put my mind to. It was her model of a servant that landed deeply in my spirit and created in me a lifestyle of servitude toward people in this present generation and in the ones to come after me. I love you, Mom, and thank you for unconditionally loving your often unloveable son. Terrell

Secondly, I am forever grateful to the mothers of my community in Granite Falls, North Carolina. You all received, corrected, and loved me as your own, and for that, I am eternally grateful. Thank you for being an extension of the hand of God toward me. I love and honor you all.

Last, but certainly not least, to you, Susan, the mother of my sons: I have always been and will forever be grateful to you for the love you have given to our children. You have nurtured and protected them; admonished, taught, and blessed them over and over throughout their lives. The seeds you have sown into them will forever bare fruit and fruit that remains. I could never fully express thanks to you for helping them to understand, appreciate, and support the call on my life as I have had to consistently fulfill the mandates of God. It has been and still is a joy to see your commitment to them as you encourage each one to be a man of influence. I acknowledge your devotion to mothering at all times in all seasons, for you started them in The Way they should go. Thank you.

FORWARD

A blessing of this impartation is that while its main focus is mothers, it's also a word of direction, encouragement, and hope to those who may be grandmothers, aunts, providers of foster care, and even mothers-to-be.

As you study these pages prayerfully, I believe you will receive insightful revelations to guide you into a greater place of confidence as it relates to caring for the children that God has entrusted to you.

Throughout this manual, Psalm 127: 3-4 will serve as the foundational scripture. Solomon pens this verse which spans generations and provides a look into the significance of the children who once graced your womb, mother.

Psalm 127:3-4

3 Behold, children are a heritage from the Lord, the fruit of the womb a reward. 4 As arrows are in the hand of a warrior, so are the children of one's youth. [AMPC]

Before we explore Psalm 127, I think it is necessary to say this. Identity is a very important thing, for in it we discover who we are, and what it is that we are to become and do in this short thing called *life*, and this shorter appointment that you have called *mothering*. The most effective thinkers are those who think in terms of generational impact. We are all called to serve our present generation with the gifts, talents, and abilities that we have in the hope that each generation will become more useful and influential in the generation of their stewardship.

You, mother, are a matriarch, yes, and that makes you powerful! My hope, throughout our time together, is that there will be an awakening that as a matriarch you have, by the sovereignty of God, been given a great responsibility; and not just to your children, but to your children's children and beyond.

That type of awareness increases according to what is called "cathedral building." It is generational building that helps to secure, preserve, and advance what is, good and useful for years to come.

One generation finds the land and plants the trees; another nurtures the trees; another cuts them down; and lastly, a generation creates the final product that is beneficial to a society.

You have been charged with training up children who will be beneficial to society. While it may have taken many years for your bloodline to get to this place, with you as that representative who is invoking change for all mothers and children who come after you; know that you are erecting something that will make a permanent impression in this world.

➤ 1

Family is everything to God.

od is the ultimate Father. He loves His children. He loves you and wants you to continue to play the critical role that you play in leading your children into destiny, which in turn will help His Kingdom to be advanced forever. Your role is extremely important. To think of creation as only the unveiling of *man* is to do a great disservice to His equally important creation in essence, which is *woman*. You, too, are made in God's image. It's not just man that was made in God's image.

God has included you in His agenda when it comes to manifesting Himself in the earth. Your role is every bit as important. When discussing creation, Adam gets most of the praise, and Eve is often viewed negatively as the one who blew it. Enough of that already, beloved daughters of God! You have God's qualities in you, too.

Beyond reproduction, you play a far more important role than that of being "barefoot and pregnant." You are more than a cook. You are more than a soccer mom. You are more than the housekeeper, who cleans the house and always knows where everything is. While all of these things are necessary and noble, never forget that **you have a divine responsibility.**

Your miraculous reproductive abilities populated the world, but beyond that, you carry influence with what God allowed or will someday allow you to partake in. That influence will impact the life He produces or will produce inside of you; and then will grace you to bring forth. I want to remind you that you do have influence with that precious seed which came from you.

And if you have lost it, I believe that it will be restored by the Lord through these anointed pages. Rejoice!

Influence is a person's ability to produce effects.

Influence effects:

- Nature
- Behavior
- Development
- Actions
- Thinking

Your son and daughter each have a nature, behavior, and development through which they must process; as well as actions and a thought life. Mom, you can and many of you do, influence all of those things. In other words, you have the divine authority to shape your child's life. And greater than that, you can guide and mold them so that the national, and even international cultures can be changed by them.

I know that sounds like a lot, but let's think from the perspective of the Kingdom of God, which transcends your home and your family alone. The mind of God wants to take you out of your city, off your street or block, and move you into a way of thinking in which most moms never engage, and that is to think *globally,* as

it relates to your child's development and potential. I am hopeful, though, that your child will be shaped by your increasing insight, revelation and perseverance to affect nations as you encounter Jesus by His Spirit in this impartation.

I'm sure that when I was growing up, my mom didn't see me as an "impactor." I exhibited a lot of negative behaviors, but somewhere in me was good seed. As that good seed was cultivated, it gave me the potential to impact the world positively. It was when I was in college smoking pot and drinking alcohol that a great aunt spoke prophetically saying that "Terrell will be the first pastor in the family." I'm sure that as she told people, they reacted just like Sarah did--behind the curtain laughing when God told her that Abraham would impregnate her at the ripe old age of 90.

After I was licensed in ministry in 1994, I served in what will be recorded in history as one of the most innovative and impactful churches in the United States:

New Birth Missionary Baptist Church. Along with its former Apostle, the late Eddie L. Long, I traveled and ministered on six continents, sat with U.S. presidents, prime ministers, and dictators; and conferred with national and international leaders. His weekly television broadcast reached millions of viewers in over 200 nations. He amassed numerous local honors and regional accolades, all to the glory of God.

In 2003 he planted me in what became one of the most influential churches in North Carolina. I am not boasting about myself here. Rather, I am beseeching you, mother, never to see your son or daughter and your relationship with them based solely on where they are, because you only see in part. I encourage you to make this declaration, **"I have the influence to shape my child's life."** Repeat it everyday for the rest of their lives. And YOU have to believe that. YOU have to believe that YOU have the influence to impact their life. YOU have to establish it in your mind that God can use you to form in them a Christlike character that will bring the Presence of God everywhere they live, work, and play.

Did Billy Graham's mom know who he was? Did Smith Wigglesworth's mom know who he was? Did Katherine Kuhlman or T.D. Jakes' moms fully know who they were? I really doubt it!

And so, when you read the Bible and you read the history of people's lives, you'll see that there weren't too many who started out and did everything wonderfully all the time. But they all have stories of challenges, and hardships, and problems. And how often do we really think that Solomon was somebody's child at one time? And so were Moses and David. The Apostle Paul and Timothy were somebody's children.

God is not a respecter of people, He is a respecter of principles, therefore, **If you take hold of God's principles, what can that child, your grandchild, your niece, the nephew of whom you have guardianship, the foster child you are training up--what can become of their life? I declare the activation of vision casting in your life for that young leader who has been placed in your care, mom. And, oh yeah...Go ahead: imagine the impossible!**

➤ 2

your child is more than cute.

he child you carried, are carrying, or will carry comes through you into a world in which he or she is more than just cute. And they are more than just smart. And on the day that you become your most upset by them, they are more than just a challenge. They are not a project or a subject in which you are trying to get an A or B. Your child is more than that, and when you begin to tap into heaven and see them for who they really are, the following things will begin to happen:

➢ You will begin to change
➢ Your children will begin to change

➢ Your relationship with your children will change

➢ As other moms witness your relationship with your child, their relationships with their children will begin to change

Whose Child Is This Anyway?

Your children belong to God, and He's equipping you to train them up in the way they should go. Scripture says in Proverbs 22:6 to *Train up a child in the way he should go: and when he is old he will not depart from it.* [KJV] Well, to do that your skill sets will have to be developed as with anything else that must be mastered. Just bringing children to church ain't enough! Really, it's not. If it were, children who grew up in church would be greater influencers of our culture.

Among children who go to church when they are in their parents' homes, 80 percent (eight out of ten), stop going to church when they leave that home! Eight out of ten! So bringing them to church is not the antidote; it's not the recipe.

So there has to be something else that mothers have to take hold of, in addition to consistently assembling their children in church.

Then what is "this way" that they should go? "This way" that they should go is God's way. We must serve them by guiding them toward a lifestyle that will accomplish God's agenda. I want to say this in a stern tone, because it is a mistake that so many parents make: God is consumed with and committed to *His* agenda for your child's life, not your agenda!

All too often parents train children to serve what *they* believe is best for their child; and too often that is far from what God created that child to pursue and live out. It's God's agenda that has to be lived out for your child's life, not yours. Your agenda must take a backseat to God's agenda. Did Mary's agenda die with Jesus? Did Hannah's agenda die with Samuel? Yes! Your agenda for your child has to die if it doesn't match God's agenda. Mom, this is a little tip with a big benefit.

Your prayer needs to be: "God, what's your purpose for this child?" And once God reveals His plans for them--and it may be over the course of many years--you can't step in and undo it no matter how much you desire something else for them. Of all the great and wonderful things your child will do in their lifetime, the thing that matters *most* is what your child does and becomes for Christ. The wrong thing will never be honored, backed, or supported by God in its fullness. God's plan for your child's life has an anointing; and any deviation will only lead to suffering, frustration, and unfulfilled purpose.

Mothers, you must side with God and tap into the anointing that moves your boys and girls into a great place in Him. That's hard, but the grace of God is sufficient enough for you (2 Corinthians 12:9). One reason it's hard is that most of us long for and pursue a better life for our children than the one we experienced. But what happens when what you want to give them that's "better" contradicts or conflicts with what God wants to do in them? Now you have to make a decision. And it needs to be a decision based on God's will. You may not know how it's going to turn out, but if you have to put the baby in a basket and float it down the river (as the mother of Moses did), then that's just what you have to do, because that's what God said do.

And while I'm sure you'd love for your child to be born in a great hospital, if you have to take him to a barn to be birthed, then that's what you have to do. That is what Mary did with Jesus because this was *God's* agenda! Mother, understand that your surrender to God's agenda, and to a greater measure of Christ's presence in your child's life will require strength and guidance. I say that because the more your decisions, attitudes, and actions reflect the mind of Jesus, (because they can be found in His Word), the more your child will gravitate to a lifestyle based on the Kingdom of God.

A child can only *be* what they see. So if they don't see you making Kingdom decisions, if they don't see you basing things on the Word of God and explaining that to them, they'll take hold of what the world is dictating for them to do; and there are plenty of opinions out there that stand diametrically opposed to the Kingdom of God. And so your determination to deny yourself will help you to train a child up who will learn self denial from you and more readily accept the agenda of God.

Once you have embraced the process of self-denial, rejecting all of the ungodly dictates of society, you now become qualified to articulate the process of living for Christ; but you can't articulate it if you haven't done it. That precious seed you have birthed can't live and carry out God's heart and God's mind if they aren't hearing you make decisions by taking up your cross; and by abstaining from unfruitful relationships, places, and things.

The sacrifices you make for the Kingdom of God are the best seeds you can ever sow into your son or daughter's life.

At 21, our oldest son has to make a lot of sacrifices now in His Christian journey. I have been blessed to witness some very strong stances he has made. I am sure that by the grace of God, they are the fruit of watching his mom and dad make sacrifices in difficult matters and rejoice in them; because while they were painful to us, they have been the way of our Lord. In his mind, what he's seen us do is live consistently as believers. We are far from perfect, but we have been graced to make incredibly difficult decisions that attest to the fact that Jesus is our Lord. He's watched us pursue the Kingdom of God all the days of his life, and that's the dominant lifestyle system that he has seen and is learning. There is a foundation that we have *intentionally* sown into both of our sons. This is our legacy.

Learn to cultivate a love for God and His Kingdom inside your child and, model that Kingdom above any other thing that you minister in their lives. I believe that the result of the time children have spent under your authority should reveal a child rooted in the Kingdom of God; and in celebration, you can look back and say, "I know my child lives with God by the fruit that is in their life."

When we are reminded of a child's life rooted in God, one of our greatest examples, other than that of Christ Jesus, is Samuel. In 1 Samuel 2:35 God says, *And I will raise up for MYSELF a faithful priest, who shall do according to what is in MY heart and MY mind, and I will build him a sure house; and he shall walk before mine anointed for ever.* [AMPC]

This is God speaking of Samuel. I am convinced that God is able to make this type of declaration because Samuel's mother, Hannah, labored in prayer over His life; and it manifested a life that was not just rooted in the Temple, but a life that was purposed for God's Kingdom. Note God says, *I will raise up for MYSELF....* He didn't say, He was going to raise up for the church, He said, *I'm going to raise up for MYSELF....* God says (paraphrased) *"I'm taking a liberty here, and this prophet, he's for ME, and he is a faithful priest."*

A prophet is one who speaks the Word and the will of God. My personal observations of the majority of our children have revealed this: our children speak the words of the city in which they live. They speak the words of the culture at the level of their engagement of it. But do they speak the Word of God? They can speak the word of a cult; they can speak the word of science; they can speak the word of technology. They can speak the word of math; they can speak the word of social networking, and they can speak the word of social trends. But can they speak the Word of God? Although they speak a multitude of languages reflecting a multitude of interests, what we should seek to develop in them is their speaking of the Word and will of God. Mom, it is the desire of God that in the likeness of Samuel, He take your child; and that child is to do according to what is in *God's heart*. Could we really be okay if our children lived doing what was in God's heart and not ours? I ask that question, because the ways of the Lord are higher than our ways.

So like Samuel's mom, Hannah, could you just leave him at the temple and turn him over--not to athletics, academics, social popularity, or even his grandmother; but release him into an environment where he gets consumed with God's way in order to become, not necessarily what *you* want him to become, but what God finds pleasing to Himself? Are you really okay with that? That can be challenging for I remember the day my mom's heart crumbled because she thought I was going to come back, after the recognition of my calling into the pastorate.

Her hope was that I would pastor Burgess Chapel United Methodist Church in Granite Falls, North Carolina, my birthplace and the place of my spiritual formation. This was *her* plan for me. But I had to follow what was in God's heart, not what was in my mom's heart. God bless Emma D. Murphy. Is it important to know and take the right course of action? Certainly, and that should be to build our children in a way that they don't mind being yielded to God. Why? Because God's loving intention is going to bring His heart and mind out of them. Mommy, I guarantee, this: the purposes of God will be good for your child, because they have been appointed to impact culture.

Write this Down: *My child is to impact the culture! That influence is not just for activists, senators, presidents, corporate CEOs, and other leaders.*

No, those aren't the only impactors of culture. It's not just doctors and lawyers, but it's boys and girls who become men and women of God.

They have a great place carved out by God as those who impact culture as well, and it's not in a natural way by power nor might, but in a supernatural way by Holy Spirit. I'm hoping to seed vision into you for what your children should be because they walk with the heart and mind of God, and that's what God is looking to raise up for Himself.

He says, in Second Samuel, *And I will build him a sure house.* It is not uncommon for a mother to feel like their house is unsure. What is an unsure house? It's when financially, relationally, and communicatively, everything is just going according to its own flow, which is actually chaotic. Now follow me, because this is how God reasons. He says, "Look, if you get your child in the right place spiritually, your child will avoid so much of what you had to deal with, because where you had an unsure house, God promises this: "I'm going to make them a sure house. But they've got to be connected to Me and realize they're Mine before they're anybody else's!"

But to succeed at this, our children have to be guarded by us in order to become sure houses, meaning that they will stay in the things of God, with our help, through love. As a child, because Jesus served in the temple, I think it can be concluded that He lived reflecting the order of God; and He was rooted in the Kingdom of God because of how He was trained up.

Matthew 6:33 says this, *But seek [or aim at, and strive after] first of all His Kingdom and His righteousness....* (AMPC)

This is what we should be building into our children. This is what they should reflect, because they have been under our authority; and they seek first the Kingdom of God and His righteousness, which is His way of doing things, and His way of being right, then ...*what they need will be added to them.*

➢ 3

The purpose of mothering

The late Dr. Myles Munroe had a conviction about which he was emphatic: *"If you don't know the purpose of a thing, you will abuse a thing."*

Let us look at **mothering** and the **purpose of being a mother**; and as we go forward, this book will serve as a means by which your mothering will not be abused or abusive, but will be enhanced as you grow in knowledge that bears eternal fruit.

<u>**Mother**</u>: A female parent; the female stewardship of parenting.

<u>**The Purpose of Mothering**</u>: Mothers are the chief exercisers of love towards children. You are often referred to as the "heart of the home."

The mother is the chief exerciser of love towards the children. If there is anyone from whom your children should receive love in its proper order and in its proper context--it should be the mother. You are the primary resource and provider of care and tenderness. I remind you, you are the chief exerciser of love. And God, by His Spirit is more than willing to show you how to exercise His love for your children through you. He is a good Father and Teacher. **Mothering is the work or skill of training up children**. (We will explore that more deeply in another chapter.)

Now as we continue to talk about the purpose of mothering, let's quickly visit the purpose of a child. A child is a son or a daughter, the offspring of a man and a woman. Remember: If you don't know the purpose of a thing, you'll abuse a thing. I have shared a little about the purpose of a child becoming a true Kingdom of God seed that infiltrates culture, but there's more to it than that. So my aim here is for you to launch deeper into understanding the value and purpose of your child.

Psalm 127 brings us into that reality. In verses three and four it says, *Behold, children are a heritage from the Lord, the fruit of the womb a reward. As arrows are in a hand of a warrior, so are the children of one's youth.* [KJV]

Children are a heritage from the Lord. Meaning they are an inheritance directly and deliberately from God. Understand this, God impregnated you with your child. You didn't think the child up! You didn't conjure the child up. God put your children inside you. Therefore, your child is an inheritance from the One who actually owns the child, and that is God. Because *children are a heritage...* that should change the way we approach our children; because we understand where they're from. And not only that, they are the *...fruit of the womb, a reward.* Every so often, I think it is a good practice to tell your child that, "You are a reward to me. There is something I did or am that God blessed me and rewarded me with you."

I believe that intimate impartations like that can help get their rooms cleaned up and dishes washed. Say to them, "Come here, my little reward!" Seriously, let your child know, "You are a reward for me, you're a reward! You weren't just plucked out of anywhere and dropped on me. You're a reward." And even if you are not the biological mother, that child was still a reward. In this scenario there's a double reward: a reward to the biological mother, and now a reward to you, because God saw fit to entrust the care of that child to you. It's all about perspective. How you see them determines how you handle them. How you see them determines how you talk to him or her.

There are times when you're mad at your child and that often creates a desire to have no communication with them and they know you're upset. Again, how you perceive them determines how you connect with them. As your anger subsides, you talk to them more, and as more anger subsides, you talk to them a little more. As your temper cools, your perception of

the child begins to change, because at the bottom of it all, your heart strings are saying, "Oh I love this child. You sure do act badly sometimes, but I love you." Your children are given to you from God. They are a reward. Now you are seeing them the right way.

The Psalmist goes on to say, *As arrows are in a hand of a warrior, so are the children of one's youth.* Your child is likened to an arrow that is to be propelled into the culture. Imagine it in this manner: Everyday you shoot your child into the culture. Everyday you shoot them into their school. What does that arrow do when it gets to school?

What it does is contingent upon what you've put into it. Then you launch them into high school; you shoot them into college; and you shoot them into the marketplace. You shoot them into marriage. You shoot them into parenthood. You even should shoot them into understanding that, "You will most likely need to take care of me one day."

That is a good mindset to shoot them into. People laugh when I say that, but I'm serious! Occasionally when I come home, my boys come downstairs and they minister to me by providing some kind of care for me. They've been trained that way.

When we go on vacation, I don't touch luggage anymore. I told them, "Your daddy is getting old, I can't be carrying all this stuff." I pull up to the gas station; they get out and pump the gas. Their mom walks up to a door and just stops, and they care for her at that point. You can't shoot them into culture and have them impact it, if there's nothing in them. Train them up in the way they should go (more on that later) so that when you shoot them into the culture, they'll reflect that training. They'll be the kid who says, "Yes, Ma'am" and "Yes, Sir." And they'll be the kid who looks people in the eye when they speak with them. And they'll be the kid who prays for people; and they'll be the one that lays hands on the sick in school during non-instructional periods, and the sick will get healed.

They'll be the one who carries the Word of God to their friends. They'll be the one who leads their friends to salvation instead of their friends leading them down paths that have no redeeming value. They'll be "The One." Whatever glorifying God is done by, "the one," they will be that one. See it, Mom. Envision it, Mom. Decree and declare it, Mom. Speak that which is not, as though it is, Mom, and thank God for it!

My primary goal, through this resource is to usher you into effective, Bible-based mothering through the transformation and liberation of your mind. I hope that has been happening thus far. Secondly, this resource is designed to help you to seed the ways of God into your child that they will live as an authentic ambassador for the Kingdom of God. Let's adjust our approach here. Internalize that you are not building your child for the university or corporate America. You are not building your child for a societal order or to "fit in.

You are building your child up to be an ambassador for the Kingdom of God. This is the highest calling.

The Kingdom of God and His servants have the highest calling in the earth. We're the only entity that has been charged with changing the world. There are many that try to duplicate us, but they cannot do it. They have a form of godliness, but they deny the power thereof. They don't have the power of the believers because we operate in the supernatural realm, and they move in the natural, earthly realm. And so we understand that our children must enter this society as catalysts who carry, provoke, and invoke change through the love of Jesus and the power of His might.

➤ 4

So where do you begin?

ive in--start where you are. Immerse yourself in this resource and allow your mind to be transformed by Holy Spirit. Confess your failures. Secondly, acknowledge your failures. No mother has been the mother that she would like to be or liked to have been. You know you've come up short in some areas. But can you confess that? Can you acknowledge that? Can you be truthful about that? It's good to be able to say "I failed. I missed the mark."

1 John 1:9 says this, *If we freely admit that we have sinned, and confess our sins, He is faithful and just, true to His own nature and promises, and will forgive our sins, [dismiss our lawlessness] and continually cleanse us from all unrighteousness, everything that is not in conformity to His will, purpose, thought and action.*[AMPC]

Confess your shortcomings to God and to your child as it relates to things that you have mishandled concerning them. Share that "I know I was wrong when I hit you with my hand, because my hand should nourish you and nurture you, not strike you." Say "I'm sorry I have spoken words that demean and disrespect you instead of edifying and encouraging you. I'm sorry I've brought things into the house--people and things that you shouldn't have seen. You've heard stuff you shouldn't have heard; and you've been around things you shouldn't have been around, because I wasn't thinking clearly, and I am sorry for that." That's where you start.

You confess your failures. And God is going to cleanse you, and He's also going to reconnect you to your child. Confess "I'm sorry that I don't listen to you and don't try to understand you. I'm sorry that when you try to talk, I talk over you. I'm sorry that I treat you like your input doesn't even matter. I'm sorry that I've talked negatively about your dad to his face and behind his back." You know where you've fallen short. Go to them and make it right. Remind yourself, 'I'm the adult.' Yes you are, so stop waiting on the child to make it right. Just go to them and fix things.

Just say, "I'm sorry I was out of line. I shouldn't have done (whatever it was.)" And when you confess, don't have an excuse. That just kills the confession. Just own it. Because somewhere it created a disconnect between you and them. A whole lot of disconnects will soon cause things to fall apart. Acknowledge and be released from any failures, any shame, and any guilt. "God, I know I missed the mark here."

Acknowledge that to God and be released from your failures. Be released from feeling like you're not good enough because you can't buy them this or that or take them here or there. Be released from that. Acknowledge those things.

"God, I've felt unfit as a mother because I haven't been able to buy my child all the things that the kids down the street are getting." Be released from that. Acknowledge strongholds in your life. "God, I'm here trying to keep up with the Jones' and they don't even know me. I'm trying to do this and do that, trying to keep up with somebody else. Now I've got the family in a financial bind." Acknowledge that and be released from it. You don't have to and you aren't supposed to be carrying all those things. They weigh you down, mother. They play on your emotions. They make you feel like you're not worthy; that you're going to fail; that you're never going to get anything done; that you're not going to do it right; and that you're not going to be good enough.

All the shame and all the guilt and all the self-condemnation-- quit turning on yourself. Let yourself go! Let yourself go! Let yourself go from guilt, shame, and condemnation. It's good to remind yourself that "I am not a failure! I did not blow it! I will not carry this shame! I will not carry this guilt! Yeah, I did it, but it's not who I am! I just missed the mark! So what?! I missed it, and I'll probably miss it again! And it's OKAY."

Why can you say that? Because you can honestly declare that **"I'm fully accepted by God! He takes my good, He takes my bad, and He takes my ugly. As a matter of fact, He's waiting on me to acknowledge that I'm held in bondage by where I came up short."** Let it go! It's not helping anything. You're not getting better in your body. You're not getting better in your mind, because you're holding on to what went wrong. Let it go! It's gone. You can't go pick it up, you can't change it, and you can't make it better! Let it go! Declare that you have power and declare you have authority!

Apostle Paul says this, *I don't consider brethren that I have captured and made it my own (yet); but one thing I do, (it is my one aspiration),* **forgetting what lies behind**. Philippians 3:13 [AMPC] (Emphasis mine.)

Can you forget? Can you say 'To heck with it!'? 'Yes, I did it, it's over, it will not hold me in bondage, it will not hold me captive.' He (Paul) says, one thing I will DO is forget what's behind me! Let us remember, this guy was killing believers, and he wrote three-quarters of the New Testament. Can't you image the attack of the adversary on his mind? I'm sure it attacked him with thoughts like, "How are you going to speak to them and you were trying to kill them? You aren't fit to talk to them! You villain! You murderer! You liar! You dawg! Look at what you did to these people! Now you're going to write a letter to them? But Paul says, "I forget about all of that!"

Forget doesn't mean to suppress, it means FORGET--forget to recall it; become unable to remember it. Paul forgets what lies behind and he presses forward to what lies ahead. So that's why you've got to get vision. You've got to get a new vision about you! Ask God to give you vision about you. Ask Him to give you vision about your children, your grandchildren, your nieces, your nephews, those for whom you're responsible.

You've got to get to a place where you get vision because the only thing that keeps you looking backwards is that you're not looking ahead!

<u>Posture yourself to mother by faith</u>: Mother by faith. The challenge for many of you as mothers is that you're waiting for your child to become or do what you fear. You're waiting on them to do "that"--the act which so antagonizes you. And all too often you find yourself preoccupied with the "bad thing" that you are so hopeful will not happen; but you give it life through your thoughts.

Worry and anxiety can actually fuel its manifestation. It's because you've learned of the negative and the alarming, and it affects how you shepherd your child.

You hear all that goes on with kids in your child's age group and so you just begin to expect "that" to happen. The "terrible twos." We wait on them. We miss the whole first year of their life waiting on the "terrible twos." Missing all of their time throughout elementary school; waiting for them to freak out in high school. Again, because you learn of the negative and the alarming, it affects how you shepherd your child. You shepherd them waiting for the bottom to fall out.

Don't wait for your daughter to come home and tell you she is pregnant. Why are you talking about that? Talk about how you are expecting to celebrate her 4.0 grade point average or GPA, and her scholarship to the college of her choice! What are we telling ourselves? What are we conjuring up in our minds?

Understand this: effective mothering is born of faith, not fear. I encourage you not to mother expecting stages of chaos and rebellion. Don't mother like that. Also expecting stages of chaos and rebellion in or from your children can keep you paralyzed and awaiting the worse. Why? Because you get what you speak!

See, the world we live in is formed by the words that we use. So if I'm speaking chaos, and if I'm expecting stages of rebellion, I'm speaking that by saying, 'I don't know what he's going to do in school. I don't even know if my son is going to get through.' Comments such as, 'I don't think my child is ever going to get a job. He is going to stay here until he is 28.' You get what you think in your heart. What does scripture say about Job? It says in Job 3:25 that *what Job feared came upon him.*

You can draw and attract negativity. You can open yourself to the spirit of fear, and it'll come in to live in you. You can open yourself up to anxiety and it will come and live in you. You can open yourself up to negativity and it'll come live in you. It will sit right down in you, and all you will do is express negativity, which feeds the negative outlook you have about your child. And you'll wonder, 'Well I don't know why they can't get it together.' Well, what have you been speaking? What have you been declaring?

Speak the positive. "My child will not repeat the seventh grade. No, my child will not fail their end-of-year tests, I don't care what it looks like! No, my child will not get anyone pregnant before they get married to them." Speak the positive. Mothers, it is time to now mother by faith and not fear.

Ted Tripp, author of the book, "Shepherding a Child's Heart," is of the same opinion. He writes this, "Most books written about teenagers presume rebellion or at least testing their limits of parental control." He says, "My assumption is the opposite..." He says, "My assumption is that you have carried out your parenting task, you've done it with integrity...."

➤ 5

Effective Mothering

ffective mothering is centered in God.

<u>Believe in God.</u> Do I really believe in God? Meaning, I take God as true, everything He says, everything He stands for, everything He's about, I take Him for true. I believe that. There's no scripture in His Word that I do not believe. There is not a promise that He says He'll perform that I don't believe that He'll perform. So this is what changes you as a mother. It is because you believe in God. He can't lie to you. He can't mislead you. He won't deceive you. I believe everything His Word says, and I follow it out.

Trust in God.

Trust in God. Believe in His ability to be reliable. Don't believe in your own ability to be reliable; don't believe in your neighbor's, but believe in God's ability to be reliable. If God rewarded you with a child, God can be relied upon to get that child to places they need to be. So you don't have to worry anymore. You don't have to be uptight. Worrying is a choice. It's a choice you make. Believe in God. Trust in God.

Rely on God.

Look to God for support. And that's not just financial support. Mental support. Physical support. Emotional support. Relational support. Look to God for support. Don't look to God for support after you've tried everything else. Don't look to God for support after everything else has let you down. But rely on God right up front. Place hope in God.

What is hope? Hope is a gut feeling that what you want is likely to happen. Place hope in God. Place confidence in God. That means 'I feel certain about God.' Why are you not drinking, crying, or losing your mind? It is because confidence in God sustains us.

Key: Faith must dictate your mothering, not fear!

You are reading this book because you are pursuing success as a mother. Not just for yourself, and this generation; but the one that is to come with the hope that your daughters will be great mothers; and that the daughters of God who marry your sons will be great mothers, too. Practice parenting that is motivated by faith. You don't want to practice parenting that is motivated by fear. Fear makes you fuss at your child. Fear makes you shut down and fall apart when your child needs you. Fear makes you doubt and worry. Fear kills your confidence in your child and separates you from God.

Lastly, you can do nothing apart from God. To provide the leadership your children need will require total connectivity and dependence on Jesus. He has brought you to this place to reveal His love to you and convey to you that in training your children up to be thought leaders and cultural impactors, you can do all things through Christ who strengthens you.

➤ 6

Leaving a Legacy

hen you were growing up how many of your parents told you that you were a heritage from the Lord? How many of your parents told you that you were the fruit of the womb, and, therefore, that you were a reward from God? When you were growing up how many of your mothers told you that you were an arrow in her hand or that she was a warrior for God? Do you remember all of these types of impartations?

With respect to your mother, it is very likely that you didn't hear these things often, if at all. It is for that reason I want to share with you why it is so important to release this type of edification to your child. It is wrapped up in one word and that word is *legacy*. Legacy in and of itself is a true catalyst that inspires expressions of comfort, belonging, and destiny to a child. And a mother who understands legacy knows that what it activates in her will change a child forever.

When you think of legacy it is normally in terms of money, property, belongings, and that is accurate. However, legacy is more specifically the passing down of or transmitting of anything from a predecessor to a successor. You are the predecessor. Your child is the successor. As a mother it is a good thing to desire to leave a legacy. It is a great accountability mechanism in your life as it compels you to govern your daily interactions deliberately and intentionally. Legacy is being formed and developed as you go through life. It speaks well of you when your time on earth has been fulfilled.

Legacy moves you to questions like:
- What type of legacy will I leave or am I leaving?
- What does my legacy look like?
- What am I bequeathing to the earth?
- What am I leaving at my job?

- What am I leaving in my neighborhood?
- How will they speak of how I conducted my affairs?
- How will I be spoken of after you leave?
- How will my life impact the generations after me?

Generational thinking is important because God is not a mono-generational God; He is a multi-generational God. He wants your life to effect the present and the next generation. None of us can say that's an unreasonable expectation. It's the DNA of our Father in heaven. Actually all of us are living our lives benefiting from men and women who invented, created, and released into the earth incredibly impactful things that are a part of their legacy. Your baby boy or your baby girl is affording you the opportunity to leave a legacy.

Often great emphasis is placed on the mother who prospers financially or who is known for her appearance or possessions; and I do applaud those things. But my heart bends toward the mother who has the reputation, above any of her marketplace accomplishments, of one who has trained up her child to live for the purposes of

God--a child who loves God because his mother has kept the example of Jesus in front of them. The mother who has made the life of Christ come alive and has nurtured a thirst for the presence of God in her child.

When you became pregnant, the legacy of child-rearing was birthed inside of you, too. You have been or will one day be given the blessing to birth a child; sow Godly principles in their heart and mind; and prepare them to create an atmosphere for the Lord wherever the soles of their feet may tread. You may not have the 5,000 square foot home, the latest luxury automobile, or access to unlimited travel and provision; but leaving a legacy that came forth out of your life by partnering with God, for the purposes of His Kingdom and His glory is far beyond the experience of tangible things which will   never last beyond your life. Oh, but a legacy--that will last throughout eternity, Mama!

Bringing correction

iversification in today's society is nothing uncommon. People hold different views toward everything and the correction of a child certainly is of high debate. Some views are so diverse and oppositional that acknowledgement or discussion is virtually taboo.

When I revisited the objective of the time that you and I are redeeming together, I knew that the matter of correction could not be overlooked. It must be addressed as a crucial part of your child's training in order for them to live in the truth of God's Kingdom and carry His glory into the earth.

How you were corrected as a child has a lot to do with how you feel about correction now as a mother. More specifically, your upbringing dictates the degree to which you seek to change your child's behavior from one form to another, and the methods you use to provoke that change. Truly some self-examination and introspection will take place as you read through this section, but it is my desire that you hear clearly what Holy Spirit is ministering to you.

It's very likely that you've wrestled with getting your child to obey you. To say that your efforts to reach a certain level of compliance to your ideal behavioral standards have been intense would undoubtedly be an understatement. As parents, you and I have expectations of our children once we have related what behaviors we consider appropriate or inappropriate. We communicate our expectations, and then look for their obedience to the acceptable behavior. Unfortunately we often encounter the exact opposite of our expressed wishes.

When our children disobey or refuse to carry out our instructions that's when the standoff begins. You see things your way, and they see things their way; and mother, they are obviously determined to win you over to their side. It is here that we have to deal with the fact that they didn't obey you. Enter correction. Keep in mind that a goal of correction is discipline. Correction means making wrong things right by removing errors in order to conform to a standard. Discipline is training, through correction which develops self-control, maturity, character, or orderliness.

Should they receive it or should they continue in their ways? If so, what should it look like, and what effect will it have on this gift of God you have been charged with nurturing, developing, and even protecting--often from themselves? This is the place, mother, where you may sometimes differ from your friends, your spouse, the child's dad, and even from God. You are often puzzled about what you should do, therefore it is imperative that you discover what the most effective correction should look like. If you seek the mind of God, your journey will lead you to a place of peace, and empower you to express love to a child who wants to avoid any level of correction, if at all possible.

I ask before we go further: What is your mindset toward correction? I just want you to ponder that question, because it will have a strong influence on how you'll accept or reject what you read. Whether you come into agreement or conflict with me, the most important thing is to trust God to open the eyes of your understanding so that in the end, you agree with Him.

There is probably less correction in the world today than there's ever been. It is because correction, even discipline, have become "dirty" words. Over the last ten years, a climate has been created in which you have to think before you speak to your child in public. People are watching the way you correct your children in those unscripted, tough moments that can manifest at anytime.

Our society is all about creating alternative words that don't come out of the heart of God. And if we're not careful, we'll adopt those alternative words instead of using words that God uses, which is where our power lies. Because we have been created in His image we, should use the words God uses, words like correction and discipline. But they're just not popular today. You can say "I did this or said that to my child," and people can look at you like you're a threat to the safety of your child.

Mothers, I know that as we have moved into this discussion, when you hear the word correction or discipline some images come to your mind. Images of things that you encountered when you were growing up. If you have not chosen to or been able to move beyond those moments, you will hear me through the pain of your experiences.

It is my prayer that you do not remain trapped in the past, but that you hear God through me and understand what He communicates, expects, and approves.

God wants you to hear in the context of His standards and divine order. I would also like to submit that you are a parent who has brought correction to your child--be it strong or light. You can't filter what I say through your means of correction, because your means could be opposed to God's. I encourage you to hear and yield to the way God wants correction applied because His way is *always* productive and fruitful.

Can I go further? Let me submit this as well:

Hearing the word correction or discipline can unfortunately serve as a reminder of brutal beatings that we received from our parents who seemed to have had no mercy at all, but believed that brutal beatings were the way to discipline. A future Hall of Fame National Football League player got suspended from play years ago because of public outrage at how he corrected his child. And he said, I paraphrase, "I beat him the way I was beat growing up."

For many of us it is difficult to talk about this issue. I encourage you to understand that unreasonable violence and brutality towards children is not biblical correction that can lead to any measure of healthy discipline. You have to give God a chance. You must not use what passed for correction in your home--actions which did not represent the Kingdom of God--as a standard to which you hold God and His order captive.

It is imperative that in your mothering you find the most effective and appropriate correction methods for your child. It is not just necessary, it is vital in order for you to guide your child into their destiny. It will assist you in establishing God's order. The less correction and discipline you bring into your child's life, the more difficult it is going to be for him or her to live as a Kingdom citizen. You will be affected by it and they will be affected by it, as will their spouses and their children.

God is a God of correction. He is a God of discipline. He is a God of love. So when we think about correction, and we think about the fruit of that correction being discipline, we have to include love as well. Correction must be centered in love. I already stated that God is love and to help us discover God's mind about correction let us look to His book of love.

Hebrews 12:1-11 *Therefore then, since we are surrounded by so great a cloud of witnesses [who have borne testimony to the Truth], let us strip off and throw aside every encumbrance (unnecessary weight) and that sin which so readily (deftly and cleverly) clings to and entangles us, and let us run with patient endurance and steady and active persistence the appointed course of the race that is set before us,*

² Looking away [from all that will distract] to Jesus, Who is the Leader and the Source of our faith [giving the first incentive for our belief] and is also its Finisher [bringing it to maturity and perfection]. He, for the joy [of obtaining the prize] that was set before Him, endured the cross, despising and ignoring the shame, and is now seated at the right hand of the throne of God. ³ Just think of Him Who endured from sinners such grievous opposition and bitter hostility against Himself [reckon up and consider it all in comparison with your trials], so that you may not grow weary or exhausted, losing heart and relaxing and fainting in your minds.

⁴ You have not yet struggled and fought agonizingly against sin, nor have you yet resisted and withstood to the point of pouring out your [own] blood.

⁵ And have you [completely] forgotten the divine word of appeal and encouragement in which you are reasoned with and addressed as sons? My son, do not think lightly or scorn to submit to the correction and discipline of the Lord, nor lose courage and give up and faint when you are reproved or corrected by Him;

⁶ For the Lord corrects and disciplines everyone whom He loves, and He punishes, even scourges, every son whom He accepts and welcomes to His heart and cherishes.

7 You must submit to and endure [correction] for discipline; God is dealing with you as with sons. For what son is there whom his father does not [thus] train and correct and discipline?

8 Now if you are exempt from correction and left without discipline in which all [of God's children] share, then you are illegitimate offspring and not true sons [at all].

9 Moreover, we have had earthly fathers who disciplined us and we yielded [to them] and respected [them for training us]. Shall we not much more cheerfully submit to the Father of spirits and so [truly] live?

10 For [our earthly fathers] disciplined us for only a short period of time and chastised us as seemed proper and good to them; but He disciplines us for our certain good, that we may become sharers in His own holiness.

11 For the time being no discipline brings joy, but seems grievous and painful; but afterwards it yields a peaceable fruit of righteousness to those who have been trained by it [a harvest of fruit which consists in righteousness—in conformity to God's will in purpose, thought, and action, resulting in right living and right standing with God].[AMPC]

So, why is it necessary to correct and discipline our children? Well, look at verse four which says it's because your children *"have not yet struggled and fought agonizingly against sin."* What our children have done is found sin, embraced sin, and walked in sin. Children, for the most part do not fight sin; they don't agonize to do right. Well, what is the result of that?

Look at Jesus, He resisted and withstood temptation to the point of pouring out His own blood. In the Garden of Gethsemane (Matthew 26:36-46) He had to make a decision: "Will I go to the cross or not?" It was the pressure, strain, and anxiety of choosing to do the right thing that caused Him to sweat*"great drops of blood."* When you go in your child's room I doubt you will find blood on the pillow from their fighting to do what is right. They are not agonizing and groaning and sweating drops of blood because they want to do right.

We have to understand that. The writer continues in verse five saying, *And have you [completely] forgotten the divine word of appeal and encouragement in which you are reasoned with and addressed as sons? My son, do not think lightly or scorn to submit to the correction and discipline of the Lord, nor lose courage and give up and faint when you are reproved or corrected by Him.*

In the context of this scripture, understand that God is talking to us as sons, as children. As you talk to your children be they male or female, you are seeing them as your son or your daughter. So He says, "My son, my daughter do not think lightly or scorn to submit to the correction and the discipline of the Lord..." (or you, mother). It is important that your children understand that you have to correct them. You have to discipline them. They must know you have to correct them and there is a reason why you have to correct them. I would encourage you to sit and share with your child why you discipline them.

Speaking from scripture is the best way to help them to understand that you have to scold them and they should submit to the correction and the discipline of the Lord, and not lose heart, become discouraged or give up and faint, because they are being reproved or corrected. Many children withdraw emotionally when they are being corrected, and seek to drive a wedge between themselves and their parents. When they're being reproved they don't want your approval, and they withdraw from you, because maybe it has not been explained to them why you have to do what you have to do as a mother who is a woman of God and who follows God.

How Do "I" Look?

Mothers, don't allow your motivation for discipline to be "You did something *to me* so I'm going to correct you." Sadly, a lot of correction comes out of this posture because when our children miss the mark, parents-- probably more times than they want to admit, (if they are aware of this at all)--immediately focus on themselves and how the child's action affects them and impacts their self-image. "How do I look now that this has happened?" Just as when the child does something good, parents reflect on "How do I look?"

Speaking pointedly, it is common for mothers to lash out, not because their child's behavior is "not the way of God," but because of how it makes the parents look. That is not the reason why God corrects. He doesn't do it because of how a child's misbehavior causes the family of God or Himself to be viewed or perceived; but He does it because of His love for the person who misses the mark. For the Lord corrects and disciplines those whom He loves.The motives for His correction are proper and are grounded in love. The Lord does it this way. Does your child know why the Lord does it this way? Or does the child know how you do it? Is your response, "Well, I'm doing what the Lord does?"

The Lord corrects and disciplines everyone He loves. Explain to your child that "The Lord does this and I have to do it, too, because I love the Lord and I love you; and

God requires of me to do what He does in correcting what is wrong." That must be the "why" of the correction, and that "why" is extremely important as the established motive of correction by a mother and father. This is the means by which the child learns of the ways of God.

Hebrew believers were Jewish believers. Proverbs 3:11 says this, *My son do not despise or shrink from the chastening of the Lord.* In the Book of Hebrews God is chastening and correcting believers for whom such correction was not a strange thing. It was something that they accepted because they knew this is what God must do. Often our children don't accept correction and discipline, because they don't know *why* you must do this. I think it is safe to say that they don't even think about it being something that is of God. They blame you. This is why we must seed the Kingdom in them so they understand and accept that correction is for their good because this is the way of the Lord. He says, ...*do not despise or shrink from the chastening of the Lord.* That's what our children have to understand.

Neither be weary or impatient; nor loathe or abhor His reproof. To make a point: Wouldn't it be an incredibly fruitful and mature statement if a child said, "Mom I know you have to correct me, and I'm ready to receive it. I know you must do this in obedience to God, because you taught me what the nature and what the character of God is about?" Children should have understanding about what you're doing. "Because I said so" is not in the Bible. I've looked for it. I started in Proverbs 31, and I did not see anywhere that the virtuous woman said, "Because I said so." That's not a scripture. And your child hasn't and never will, nor will their children receive "Because I said so" as an acceptable response.

For whom the Lord loves... (Proverbs 3:12) He does what? *...He corrects.* Even as the Father God does, mother, correct the son in whom you delight. Correction is a part of the Kingdom of God. To exclude it is to be outside of the Kingdom. Failure to correct and refusal to discipline a child is to live in subjection to another system--the world's system. That system says, "Let the child go.

Let children explore and learn for themselves." How's that workin' for ya? It ain't!

God is showing us through these scriptures that correction and discipline are far from dirty words. As much as the politically correct agenda would love for you to do so, you don't have to tread lightly, using euphemisms when talking to your coworkers, because you're unsure how they might respond if you say that you correct and discipline your child. You can speak freely because they are biblical terms, and they are a part of our Kingdom. When you consistently discipline your child, and do it with the right attitude, you are expressing the love of God to your child.

This means your own actions are compassionate and controlled. You set realistic, consistent boundaries; you expect realistic, consistent consequences; and you are focused on the child's best outcome. But the child must *understand* that you are doing this to get the best outcomes for them because you love them. It's okay to be compassionate about your correction, just make sure it is under control; and be intentional about it, setting consistent boundaries.

> ### ➤ Compassionate Correction

Correction that is sorrowful for the suffering or trouble of the one being corrected.

> ### ➤ Correction Under Control

Correction that is Bible-based which directs the action of the one exercising the authority to correct.

> ### ➤ Correction/Consistent Boundaries

Correction that is consistent with the expressed correction; measured by type of correction; length of correction, and that always provokes behavioral change.

Again, the correction must focus on the child's best outcome, not on your need to feel relieved that you were able to correct them. The object must always be that the good fruit of that correction is realized. It must be about the best outcome for the child. Correction may seem uncomfortable for both of you at the time, but in the long run it's the most selfless, compassionate thing you can do to set your child up for happiness in life and fruitfulness.

I was Punished

Your style of correction as a parent is a reflection of the correction you received as a child. I'd like to add another character to the discussion: punishment. I think it's safe to say that what the majority of you received as children was punishment. It is usually the way for those who receive a thing to pass that same thing along. I think that punishment is the ugly legacy disguised as correction which has been passed to most children. Correction and punishment bring different results. They form different mindsets and different attitudes in your child.

When does punishment show up? Punishment is certain to rear its head when, as parents, we feel our child has betrayed, embarrassed, and offended us. We become wounded by their disloyalty and are frustrated by repeated disappointments. Often our response to their behavior is an emotional one and we punish the child for the anguish they've caused us. The closer the relationship; the more sacrifices you make; the more of yourself you invest in your child's life, the greater the tendency to retaliate and punish your child when they are out of line.

It works like this: Because you feel betrayed; because

you feel your daughter or son has been disloyal or has deceived you; lied to you, or conspired against you behind your back, you strike back. Your response is an emotional one: "Now I'm going to punish you for what you did."

Unknowingly, punishment becomes the primary reaction because we forget about the mercy of God. When you forget about applying the mercy of God, you can bet that someone is going to be punished. Mercy is often downplayed as "too soft," the fear being that mercy won't convey what really needs to be communicated; therefore by default, punishment becomes the preferred response. Punishment teaches your children that they need to be paid back for the bad things they've done. Really?

Let's look at it this way. Christ died for your children's sins, too. But do we think about that when we have to "lovingly" confront them? It's true, He died for the sins of the world, which includes your child. Jesus died for your child's sins, too. The price has been paid. However, you may (and I'm sure it is a subconscious goal) still want to make them pay.

Should they have to pay again when the price has already been paid? That is what punishment does. Through punishment, we actually start to undo the work of atonement that Jesus accomplished at Calvary. Many mothers forgive their child *after* the spanking, or *after* telling them off. They've already been forgiven for what was done because of Jesus, but our conformity to the patterns of correction and punishment we endured as children compels us to do as our parents did.

Forget mercy and just punish them!

Like our parents, we demand payment, because if you do wrong, you're going to pay for it. And what is more scandalous is that we chose severe methods and measures of payment designed to please ourselves, regardless of the outcome for the child. But the price has been paid! If Jesus took all the punishment for you and me, He took it for them, too. Your child does *not* have to be to punished. Why? Because Jesus took their punishment on

Himself. You shouldn't have to make your child go through what Jesus has already endured and spared them, which is punishment. Praise God!

8

Giving Appropriate Consequences.........

I believe the Spirit of God would want you to move in this manner. Consider it: Mother, it is not your role to punish your child. Rather, your role is to provide appropriate instructions that lead to appropriate consequences so that they can see how their behavior pleases or displeases who? God! Appropriate instructions and appropriate consequences are essential if we are to reveal how God sees and reacts to their behavior. So we do what? TEACH them to cooperate with God's work in their lives.

You are your child's trainer and equipper. You are the Apostle of your house. That's your church there. I encourage you to provide appropriate consequences for their misbehavior, and then instruct them so that they see how displeasing that was to God. Not to mom.

This is what the Bible calls discipline. This is how discipline looks in the Bible. It's all about God's displeasure, not mother's. It's about correcting them, and not punishing them, so that their appreciation for God's love is nurtured in their heart. Love is key. It should be their love for God that causes them to yield to the work of His Spirit in their lives, which ultimately brings to bear His likeness and His image in a new generation of believers who no longer despise His correction.

Punishment Produces:

- Guilt

- Shame

- Bitterness

- Resentment

- Regret

- Self-pity

- Fear

Punishment produces, guilt, shame, bitterness, resentment, regret, self-pity, and fear. Why does it do that? Because it focuses on the past! Children feel helpless, because they can't undo what they've already done. When the tendency is to remind them of how bad they **were**, they often feel ashamed and guilty; and then bitterness towards you, other people, and even authority figures begins to fester in their heart and manifest in their life.

Punishment does not give children the tools to right their wrongs. For the large majority of children, correction involves some form of punishment, which keeps them from seeing and experiencing the love of God. It actually creates bondage. If someone commits a crime, comes into the courtroom, and is found guilty, they cannot go back to the scene of the crime and make that right. They go straight to jail. When your child can't make things right--by their own will--because they're punished, they're now in jail. They are now locked up.

Children know that they were not made for prison, and it is here that the spirit of rebellion enters, because punishment leads them into a place of insecurity, and ineffectiveness, because they cannot right the wrong.

Imagine the psyche of a child who cannot fix what they have done wrong or doesn't even have the opportunity to. The economy of the Kingdom of God provides repentance. When we confess our sin, "God is faithful to forgive us of our sins and cleanse us from all unrighteousness."(1 John 1:9) [KJV] Correction is not all retribution and no redemption. Retribution means you start paying the price right now. You did this. Your punishment is to pay this price. You did that. Your punishment is to pay that price. And there is no redemption. There is no freedom. When Jesus died on the cross, He redeemed us, and set us free; and He keeps us in right relationship with Himself through forgiveness.

I shared the results of punishment earlier. The result of correction is security. God-ordained correction will communicate to a child that they are loved. It says, "You are still okay with me." Punishment means I have to go through an extended period of separation from you or things with which I have been blessed, because you are angry with me. In our young kids, this is how they begin to feel insecure about their lives, and hidden under that contemplation is the question, "Am I any good?" "Sure you are!" That may be your answer. "So why am I locked up?" they ask. A locked-up inmate does not feel like a contributor to society; likewise, a child who is serving a sentence doesn't feel like a useful member of the family. Correction that leads to discipline is always focused on the child's best interests, not the parent's anger. Godly correction is never out of control. Punishment, however, gets out of control.

Parenting Myth About Correction

➢ Myth

Correction requires parents to penalize their child as payback for an offense.

➢ Reality

Correction requires applying appropriate instructions and consequences to encourage a child to make better choices in the future. Correction makes things that are wrong, right. It is applying appropriate consequences; that's why parenting has to be Holy Spirit-led. The Spirit of God should direct the consequences you select, not your wounded feelings. It is not good to draw conclusions based on your soul (mind, will, and emotions). Spirit-led decisions will express the mind of God and inspire the application of appropriate instructions and consequences to encourage a child to make better choices in the future. Let's go a little further.

Correction should be with both action and words. Correction is very controversial, and the general consensus is it should only be applied punitively or in an injurious manner. A lot of people don't talk about how they correct their children, because of cultural taboos and societal biases which could easily result in your losing custody of your child. Correction is rarely presented as the rational act of a responsible parent; rather it is regarded as an extreme measure.

9

God, what do you say about this?

Proverbs 13: 24 sheds great light on this matter from God's perspective. Paraphrased, it says, *"He/She that spareth his rod hateth her son, but he who loveth him chasteneth him betimes."* If you love your child you're careful to correct them. If you love your child you will not spare the rod. Proverbs 22:15 is the reason that a rod is God's chosen instrument for correction. It is because *Foolishness is bound in the heart of a child, but the rod of correction shall drive it away from him.* [KJV] This is the Word of God.

A Rod? Really?

I promote Christian, biblical parenting. The lifestyle of a believer is lived out of their heart. It is from the heart that the life of Christ is demonstrated and it is from a heart of love that correction should be administered. God's image should be reflected in all mothering. Correction is not an action that strives to conform behavior, but to adjust the attitude of a child's heart. The goal of corrective actions based upon Christian parenting is to train the heart of a child to reflect Christ.

The context of a rod is of high importance here. Children are not born morally or ethically neutral. The Bible teaches that the heart is "deceitful and desperately wicked" (Jeremiah 17:9) [KJV]. Your child does not have an information deficit; the problem is that they sin. The "rod" is cited because it can meet certain needs within a child. Folly is in their hearts and cannot be talked out, therefore God says drive it out with the "rod."

Children have hearts of folly. They resist correction and authority, and seek to live driven by their own wants and passions. God has, therefore, devised the "rod" to drive out foolishness. Disobedience brings your child into the place of physical and spiritual death. Mom, I know you have felt like this before: you are charged to rescue your child from death—it may be often. The rod is a *biblical* tool for that rescue. *A rod and a reprimand impart wisdom, but a child left undisciplined disgraces its mother....17 Discipline your children, and they will give you peace; they will bring you the delights you desire.* (Proverbs 29:15,17) [KJV]

The rod is not a "go to" weapon. Being transparent, even I had to come to this realization in the correction of my children. The rod is what needs to be applied when a child is exhibiting behavior from which they need to be rescued. This is usually the case where rebellion and stubbornness have been identified and addressed, but no fruit of transformation has come forth. For a child to continually and consistently choose their will over God's, they need to be forcefully brought back under the authority of God and their parents.

The website **Capitolhillbaptist.org** suggests that the rod of correction brings wisdom to a child by:

> ➢   Providing an immediate tactile demonstration of the consequences of rebellion, and;

> ➢   Imparting to the child a Godly fear of rebellion and a proper fear of correction.

Properly administered biblical discipline applied with the rod teaches the child that rebellion yields only trouble; and it humbles the heart of a child, bringing him back under parental instruction.

What is the rod? The resource above defines the rod as: **The rod is a parent--living in Godly faith and faithfulness toward his or her children--undertaking the responsibility of careful, timely, measured and controlled use of physical correction to underscore the importance of obeying God, in order to rescue the child from continual foolishness unto death.**

Earlier, I said that all correction should be Holy Spirit-led, wherein the parent is prayerful and completely yielded to acting according to the Holy Spirit's wisdom. *If any of you is deficient in wisdom, let him ask of the giving God [Who gives] to everyone liberally and ungrudgingly, without reproaching or faultfinding, and it will be given him.* **(James 1:5)[AMPC]**

The rod (spanking) involves a level of severity which should be used properly and sparingly. I would recommend that you hold yourself accountable to a trusted, Spirit-led confidante regarding how and why you enforce rod correction before and after each incident. You won't need to spank your child throughout his childhood, especially if you do it appropriately and consistently early in their life. At certain ages it is the most appropriate, effective, and compassionate approach you can take. Our sons were not spanked a lot from the age of nine through their teenage years.

I believe it was because the rod of correction they received as toddlers instilled in their hearts a reverence for God, and respect and honor for us as their parents; and levels of wisdom were sowed into their spirits.

When correcting them with the rod we were not angry, out-of-control parents who were venting their anger and exercising no prudence. The tendency is to withhold this type of correction because of what we experienced at the hands of our own parents. Well, maybe your parents were out of control because that was all they knew. You have to judge that. Perhaps they drank, but you don't have to drink because they drank. Maybe they smoked, but just because they smoked, you don't have to smoke. If they were unable to keep a job, you don't have to suffer periodic unemployment. So just because your parents corrected incorrectly, it doesn't mean that you have to correct incorrectly.

All correction of your child should be done in love, be sealed in prayer with you and your child; and end with a time of restoration that reinforces your love for your child, so that they are able to move forward with a clear conscience regarding their indiscretion. When it's experienced in this manner, it's healthy, for it follows the corrective order of God for His creation.

When you do wrong, God's love convicts you. He reasons with you, forgives you when you repent; and then you can come boldly to the throne of grace to obtain mercy and grace to help you in your time of need--your time of restoration. You can then be restored, and allowed to proceed with a clear conscience; because once you have reasoned together, you can see the error of your ways.

Can you see how different that is? It is not fair to a child for you to correct them by word, but especially by the rod, and pour no love, relational, or pastoral care into their heart. Then we wonder why they are bitter. It is because they just got rebuked, and most likely punished, and without the healing balm of reconciliation. They cannot 'just get over it,' and be okay. "Better tuck that lip back in before I spank you again!" WHAT?!? "Now get down there and eat!" EAT?!?!

I hear your child saying "Why don't you love me right now? You were mad enough to correct me! Why don't you love me enough to comfort me?!" The importance of what I am saying is that it helps to build a healthy intimate relationship between you and your children.

$\succ$ 10

what doesn't work

A battle that is waged by yelling **and screaming is not an effective means of correction at all.** No good can come out of that, especially, when your kids learn to yell back--and they will. Why? Because you have taught them that what you do when you get upset is to yell, so they will yell back.

Unclear boundaries and mixed messages damage a child's ability to adjust to correction. Clear, consistent boundaries teach them what they can and can't do, and if there are changes, you have to explain it to them.

Timeout is another form of correction that is very popular among parents. Here is the challenge: Timeouts are a slower, more drawn out process. My concern here is that it creates periods of isolation in which the child is "left to themselves" after being confronted about a wrongdoing. So if you tell your child to go face a corner, the time in the corner will become a gateway to anger, misunderstanding, offense, and bitterness among other evil antagonizers. These demonic forces can now fill both the corner and the child with the thoughts and feelings of the Antichrist while they "wait" on you for release. It is best to have the soul and spirit of a child cleansed immediately.

Slapping and Hitting.

STOP THAT CYCLE! It's abuse. If you have not started, DON'T START IT! Bottom line. The rod, according to scripture, is the only acceptable physical method of correction--not slapping, punching, kicking, or throwing things at them.

Correction for Kingdom Advancement

When you look at First Samuel it reveals a lesson that lends validity to the importance of correction. It's worth the labor of love. Mom, correction requires consistency, wisdom, discernment, and obedience to God. It is another part of our spiritual responsibility towards our children that we need to carry out. When you look in First Samuel you see the bad results of Eli, the priest and father who refused to correct and discipline his sons. They were at the temple seducing young women and stealing money because the only thing he said to them was "Stop."

Eli did not execute any level of correction against them. And these boys' disobedience escalated into an act desecration when they took the Ark of the Covenant of God out of the temple and into battle. They took it into war with them, believing that if they brought "The Presence" with them they would have victory. Their growing, unchecked disobedience devolved into prostituting The Presence of God in order to get a Godly result in a place where God wasn't working.

He never stopped his sons. So they went from disobedience, to seduction, to stealing, to false worship. How did this happen? Because all their God-appointed guardian said to them was "Stop." "Stop" isn't enough. You have to explain; you have to communicate; you have to do what is appropriate according to what the Spirit of God is telling you to do where your children are concerned.

Desire to train up a child who bares righteous fruit and who will live with lasting joy. It is by the spirit of God that Godly correction brings Kingdom fruit and righteousness. Your child is a reward from God and if you have been able to establish proper order through appropriate correction, then I encourage you to continue in what is bearing fruit. But if you have met with resistance and frustration, I say that you are well able to reenter the sensitive arena of correction with your son or daughter; and I am confident that the revelation you have received here will reap a harvest and manifest victory for you and your children, for you are more than a conqueror!

Correcting is Serving

I stated earlier that mothers should serve their children in a manner that will accomplish God's agenda. I believe it is an incredibly rewarding approach. Imagine that: being a servant to your child. Of course, I'm not talking about "Hey ma, can you get me some water and bring it upstairs." That's probably going to take us back to the section on correcting your children.

I'm talking about serving them to deliver them into their destiny; serving them so that they come into a place in the Kingdom of God where the fruit of their life is so rooted in God that you know you have a child who will follow the ways of the Lord. This is not a fly-by-night concept producing temporary results; for it involves applying some very singular and significant precepts that I will lay out for you. Application has as its root, the word apply which means "to put on or spread on." It is to "place something so as to be touching it." So what I encourage mothers to do daily is to apply, or put the Kingdom of God on your child--actually spreading that onto your child's life. You're permeating your home with it. Your whole family will know how to live a lifestyle that creates an eternal, healthy, significant relationship among siblings; spreading it on so that they would be honorable to their parents, their grandparents, and their extended family.

Spreading it on gives them instructions and directions about how they should behave in the neighborhood; how they should socialize at the park; how they should engage the public on family outings; how they should be in school or afterschool; and how they should be as they're navigating through life--you are spreading it on them. Picture yourself spreading butter on a piece of bread with a knife. See it? Okay, that's you spreading the anointing of God all over your child's life. So what? So that the Kingdom begins to manifest "out of them."

So Let's Get To Spreadin'

The first thing that you have to do is be available to them. That is so important for your child: be available to them. Let's bring some clarity to this. Just because you're in the same room, doesn't mean you're available. Let's get a clear picture of what **being available** looks like. Our greatest example of this is found in **Deuteronomy 6:6**. the Word of the Lord says, *"...and these words which I am commanding you this day shall be first in your **own** mind and in your **own** heart."* [AMPC]

He says first, mothers, that this has to happen in **your own mind and in your own heart**. God is commanding that the Word must first enter into the mind and heart of a mother before it can enter into a child's life. In love, I challenge you to take new scriptures **into** your heart weekly. 'Taking into' implies, not just memorizing, but activating it in your life. To know is to do. If you are doing a Word, it is reflected by the fact that you do that Word. The more of God's Word that you take into your own mind and heart, the more it impacts you and all the things in which you engage. There are words of God, scriptures, mother, that you can begin to internalize that will translate into a healthier relationship between you and your child in every area of your lives.

Once you take it into your own mind and heart, it can be taught, expounded upon, and relayed to your child with understanding. God says it like this in **Deuteronomy 6: 7**: *"You shall whet and sharpen them (the word you have taken into your own mind and heart) so as to make them penetrate and teach and impress them diligently upon the minds and hearts of your children and shall talk of them when you sit in your house, when you walk by the way and when you lie down and when you rise up."* [AMPC]

If you did that for an entire year you would be Mom-of-the-Year, well, in your household at least. "I'm Mom-of-the-Year." Well, who voted for you? "My children voted for me." You have to believe that the Word works and that the Word is valuable. You have to be convinced that you can't live without the Word of God.

The two most powerful things in the world are:
> ➢ Men's needless traditions, and *the Word of God.*

Accomplishment and progress in your parenting will come from the Word of God being received and believed in your own heart and your own mind. Now, as scripture says, "You shall whet and sharpen them so as to make them penetrate." What you say to your child--that is, the Word of God and His principles which come out of you-- should penetrate their spirit, body, and soul. God's work in their lives.

➤ 11

Connecting by the word of God

Discernment will help you bear fruit as you seize divinely anointed opportunities to take God's Word and principles and impart them into your child. An effective application strategy is to introduce and discuss a specific biblical principle; and then, as you discern that your child is beginning to connect with that principle on some level, and to "buy into" it, mention the particular scripture and its exact location in the Word. To mention a principle and get the attention of your son or daughter, and then navigate to the scripture shows the child that the principle is in this incredibly powerful thing called the Word of God and let them see it for themselves.

So what are you doing now? You're penetrating and teaching and you're impressing the Word upon your child. You are spreading it on diligently. Mom, it's a good thing for you to take the Word of God and have consistent Bible study with your child, not just when they make a mistake, but at every available opportunity. When divine opportunity knocks, make it relevant to their day at the nursery; make it relevant to their time on the baseball field; make it relevant to what they were dealing with in school. Make it relevant to whatever is going on in their lives. Making it relevant to their world will help them grasp it and apply it.

Moms, I know this may seem burdensome, adding yet another task to your busy schedule, but this task is a divine calling that will bring the nature of Jesus to bear in your children.

Teach the Word to them. Get It in their minds and their hearts. That takes a lot of work, but instilling Christlikeness is well worth it. Faith comes by what? Faith comes by hearing and hearing and hearing and hearing.

I don't recommend speaking the Word in anger because you risk presenting the Word in a very negative light. You could turn the Word into a weapon against which your child's heart may harden. We must put a greater honor and value on the Word than that. Speak the Word into them in love while you're training them.

12

Making Time

By now I think that we have developed a level of relationship and inspired enough trust for me to say some tough things that need to be said. Do you want to regain your title of Mom-of-The- Year? Then let's deal with your TV time; your mani-pedi time; and your phone time. Regarding all of your "me time" and everything else you do in your house--I'm about to get into it. God says in Deuteronomy 6 that you shall **talk** to them, not ignore them; not put them in front of a television set and let it babysit them; not impatiently bark, "Do as I say!"

He says you are to talk about the commandments of the Lord when you sit in your house. He clearly states that a majority of conversation must be of the things of God-- not foolishness or nonsense; not TV shows and gossip. No, those things have very little redeeming value. Instead, talk about the Word of God when you sit in the house with them. Of course, this means that if you are not taking time to sit, I encourage you to start taking time to sit.

I remember a football game my son wanted to attend. I really didn't want to go to the game because it was going to rain. Again, I didn't want to go, but I realized it would give me the chance to spend time in the car with him. I had to recognize that from God's perspective, it was an opportunity to talk with him. My posture was to listen to him, and whenever a case for the Kingdom needed to be imparted, I would do that (principle then scripture).

Often opportunities to connect are not easy, therefore be led by the Spirit of God to incorporate divine dialogue into everyday conversations. Be deliberate about making the most of your God-ordained time together. Move past disagreements. Don't sit, walk, or ride together, and be mad with them. Don't sit on the phone gossipping, murmuring, or complaining. Be careful to season your conversation with love and compassion. All conversations are not appropriate for them, and they are most likely hearing inappropriate things you may be saying.

Take that time to turn the radio off, unless you're listening to a spiritual broadcast together, or you're listening to a leadership CD together which will help you develop their leadership skills. God would have you teach and impress upon your child's spirit wholesome ideas, beliefs, and values. He says do it when you **sit** in your house, and when you **walk** by the way, and when you **lie** down, and when you **rise** up. That may seem like a "whole lot of talkin'" about the things of God, but the takeaway from God's perspective is that almost your entire life should be consumed with you pouring into your child the awesome things of God. This not overkill. This is a matter of life and death. We are at war.

We wage spiritual battles each day, and mothers, it is required that you seed into your precious gift to prepare them to stand against the onslaughts of this ungodly society. I believe that it is important to reassess your availability to your child. If you are in the house with them, are you really *with* them? I know that you can't be with them every single moment you are in the house, but you have to be cognizant to ask, "Why am I just leaving them to themselves for these four or five hours and not checking on them?" I believe that Hannah was intentional about engaging what God called a faithful priest (1 Samuel 2:35). When you read Deuteronomy 6:7 you'll see that it is really the foundation for teaching and guiding your child. **Teach and Guide.** For every area of their lives you must teach and guide. Look for opportunities to teach and guide them.

> 13

Proverbs 31 Mothering

et Involved. No person, including your child, is the same way all of the time. Nor can you approach them the same way all of the time. Learning the most effective approach for any given situation is the best way to stimulate fruitful conversation. (A key to the effectiveness of connecting is to remember how you did it.) Remembering *how* you connected is going to greatly increase the effectiveness of your involvement in your child's life.

One of the most notable women of the Bible is the featured matriarch of Proverbs 31 who has been deemed *The Virtuous Woman.* She is full of wisdom and she carries virtue that allows her to be an excellent role model because of her ability to speak in the proper manner. Remember this: **Take right approaches to create long lasting involvement.**

Proverbs 31:26

She opens her mouth in skillful and godly wisdom and on her tongue is the law of kindness giving counsel and instruction. [AMPC]

The writer points out a key to her success: when she opens her mouth she's being "skillful." She's developed a skill set that tells her how to speak and what to say. What elevated her to this level of insight and discernment? She carries Godly wisdom. Your daily involvement in your child's life requires skillful, discerning interaction. There is no time for foolish, futile discussion that is devoid of edification and meaning. It needs to be skillful. The virtuous woman opens her mouth in skillful and Godly wisdom.

She doesn't talk about things that have no eternal value, she doesn't talk people down. If she must speak against another person's actions, she does so with Godly wisdom.

Skill is the ability to do something well. Wisdom is key because it knows the end from the beginning, and reveals the best route to get there. The skillset of the virtuous woman in Proverbs 31 was entirely centered on and shaped by wisdom. To this woman God revealed things that He hid from others. She was anointed by Godly interaction to speak at a level of wisdom which manifested changes in the lives of others. Her approach was always Spirit-led, not irrational, fleshly, or emotional.

Even in the heat of a moment, children need to be the recipients of skillful engagement, not emotional tirades in which you impulsively "shoot from the hip." In all situations there are a lot of things you may want to say, but is the law of kindness, according to Proverbs 31:26, on your tongue? Will your words give counsel or instruction? This is the way of the Lord.

Sadly and even unwittingly, some mothers taught their daughters how to cuss, how to murmur, and how to backbite. They taught their mothers and wives-to-be how to be double minded; how to smile in a person's face and then talk about them behind their back. None of that is skillful or edifying. None of that is born from Godly wisdom. These mothers probably were never taught what should be on their tongues.

Words are life. They should convey kindness. Words provide good counsel. Words give instruction. The law of kindness will serve you as a catalyst to serve your child. It can forge an enduring relationship and long lasting involvement in their life. Involvement leads to interaction, discussion, and collaboration as they process challenges and make important decisions. All of that is involvement.

From a practical sense, maybe playing solitaire will open the door to deeper interaction. Perhaps, going to the restaurant *they* like will create an opportunity for involvement with them. You may hate the restaurant, don't want to be in it, can't stand it, but it's where *he or she* wants to be. You are not after a five-star dinner experience, you are after your child's heart. With that in mind, it makes better Kingdom-sense to go to the place of their choosing and get involved. You are a seed sower, and because you are sowing good seed you should expect "good" to come up.

➢ Teach Them

2 Timothy 3:16

Every Scripture is God-breathed (given by His inspiration) and profitable for instruction, for reproof and conviction of sin, for correction of error and discipline in obedience, [and] for training in righteousness (in holy living, in conformity to God's will in thought, purpose, and action).... [AMPC]

Every scripture is God-breathed and given by His inspiration. Now think about your child and what they need because the Word of God is profitable for instruction.

It's profitable for:

- ➢ Reproof
- ➢ Conviction of sin
- ➢ Correction of error
- ➢ Discipline
- ➢ Obedience
- ➢ Training in righteousness, and holy living, and conformity
- ➢ Helping people move into God's will in thought, purpose, and action.

These things are what the Word of God does. Children should be taught the Word of God because all of the things listed above--when experienced in love--are for the good of your child. This is what Samuel looked like. This is what seeking the Kingdom of God looks like. Every scripture is necessary, so it's advantageous to lead your child to them. There are enumerable things that your child encounters daily, but none is greater than the Word of God. There is a Word to go with that child and all they may face each day.

Even if he or she is young (a toddler or of elementary school age) you should still speak the Word into that child. Help them to understand what the scriptures mean. It is a great practice to ask a child to explain what a scripture means and how they can use it for their lives in a given situation.

Teach them scriptures; and teach them a biblical worldview, which is simply this: **Making sense of the world from the perspective of God.** Everything else is coming at them forcing them to make sense of the world according to personal and political agendas that organizations, institutions, and special interest groups are pushing. These groups are flooding the airwaves with what they feel. They are advancing their philosophies, and our children are gaining a perspective of things that come from the world and not from the Bible.

A mother who knows, or who is teachable, can take their child to the Word of God and help them to understand God's mind. If this is or becomes your practice, stick with them until they gain understanding.

Help them get the understanding of a matter and why it is right or wrong in the economy of God.

Things like:

➤ This is why God created a Kingdom.

➤ This is why this family goes to church and what it means to God.

➤ This is why and how God honors generous giving.

➤ This is why God wants you to grow up and serve in the church.

➤ This is why the pursuit of purity is important to God.

➤ This is God's way that marriage should look.

➤ This is why when you grow up, God wants you to train your children up in the way they should go.

Children need to discover, through parental guidance and through the Word, the difference between God's Kingdom and its citizens, and the world and its citizens. Your child thinks that they're the center of the world, because they lack a biblical worldview. They think everything should revolve around them, because they don't understand that it revolves around God.

It's *all* about God. And the sooner your child understands that there is a God, and that He has a Kingdom; and that the earth and all that is in it comes from Him, the sooner they'll begin to discover just how big and great God is! As they begin to understand that all things revolve around God, and nothing goes on that He doesn't know about, including everything they need, they will begin to open up to His sovereignty and love.

Luke 12:56 says "You play actors hypocrites you know intelligently how to discern and interpret and approve the looks of the earth and sky but how is it that you don't know how to **discern and interpret and apply the proof to this present time?**" [AMPC] Our children need to have a biblical worldview. Their knowing Mozart and every rapper, and every entertainer, and what every car is, and what every designer is, and so many things they're inundated with does not help them to discern the present time. Jesus, in Luke 12:56, was telling those who were standing around that you know everything that's going on, you know what happens when the sky changes colors; you know all of those things, but you can't even give me a biblical worldview about what is going on in this present time. You don't want your children to be ignorant of the devil's devices in the earth. (2 Corinthians 2:11)

➤ 14

Train them up in the way they should go

Proverbs 22:6 *Train up a child in the way he should go [and in keeping with his individual gift or bent], and when he is old he will not depart from it.* [AMPC]

The way that your children should go is the way of the Kingdom of God. As their Creator, He knows their gifts— natural and spiritual (**1 Corinthians 12:11**).The sovereignty of God pertaining to your child is a sure thing. Jeremiah 1:5 points to just that fact. It declares that ,*"Before I formed you in the womb I knew [and] approved of you [as My chosen instrument], and before you were born I separated and set you apart, consecrating you; [and] I appointed you as a prophet to the nations."*

Before your child was even formed in your womb, God had set him or her apart for a specific purpose. He gave them a bent and then, as 1 Corinthians 12:11 points out, He holds onto spiritual gifts that He--in accordance with His own will and timing--releases into them. This will prepare your child to walk in things for which He has set them apart. Later on in the same context, He says in Jeremiah 29:11, "For I know the thoughts *and* plans that I have for you, says the Lord, thoughts *and* plans for welfare *and* peace and not for evil, to give you hope in your final outcome." [AMPC] This is the sovereignty of God toward your child.

To discover the specifics of what "the way" is in the Kingdom of God will certainly require prayer and fasting in the confidence that God will reveal the plan, and guide you as you lead your child on the path that God has for them. This, mom, is not an easy task, but it is part of your job description as a mom. You are your child's greatest intercessor.

In Matthew 6:10 the disciples pray, "Your kingdom come, Your will be done on earth as it is in heaven." Their desire was God's Kingdom and God's will in their lives. This should be the shared desire of all mothers: to know what the will of the Lord is for their child. First Corinthians lends itself to this fail-proof model and **Ephesians 5:15-17** admonishes you to *"Look carefully then how you walk! Live purposefully and worthily and accurately, not as the unwise and witless, but as wise (sensible, intelligent people). Making the very most of the time [buying up each opportunity], because the days are evil. Therefore do not be vague and thoughtless and foolish, but understanding and firmly grasping what the will of the Lord is."*[AMPC] (Emphasis mine.)

Children are trained in a lot of things that are not aligned with God's perfect will for them. This does not mean that the wholesome things they may be trained in are not good. I was trained athletically most of my life and played football throughout college. However, it was not the dominant purpose of my life.

Other things were a part of my journey, but when the purpose of my life was revealed, I stopped allocating time for things that were not good for me. I began embracing things that would guide me into "the way" that God had ordained for me before He formed me in my mother's womb.

A lot of people discover their dominant assignment ultimately, but the time, money, and energy that are expended because "the way" was not discovered years before or thousands of dollars earlier can never be regained. It is not the will of the Lord for you to waste your time, or energy, nor your child's time or energy. God's way, which holds "the way" for your son or daughter is precise, and the discovery of it and its benefits to your child reap eternal blessings.

I leave you with the following. Trust it and help your child to know and trust it:

Lean on, trust in, and be confident in the Lord with all your heart and mind and do not rely on your own insight or understanding. In all your ways know, recognize, and acknowledge Him, and He will direct and make straight and plain your paths. (**Proverbs 3:5-6**) [AMPC]

➤ Instill The Fear Of The Lord

Proverbs 1:7

7 The reverent and worshipful fear of the Lord is the beginning and the principal and choice part of knowledge [its starting point and its essence]; but fools despise skillful and godly Wisdom, instruction, and discipline.[AMPC]

How your child sees God will forever have an impact on their success in life. God loves us and desires to be loved by His creation. Solomon, the writer of this Proverb, writes it to teach young men knowledge and discretion. He bases this on two fundamental laws of morality:

1. Children should regard God as Supreme.
2. Children should have high regard for parents as their superiors.

➤ Children Should Regard God as Supreme

Solomon lays down this truth, that the fear of the Lord is the beginning of knowledge; it is the principal part of knowledge; and it is the head of knowledge. Children should know that above all things: God is to be feared, reverenced, served, and worshipped. This is key for your child. If there is anything to know, then this is it.

Children develop many mindsets, but unless those mindsets include a holy reverence for God, then every thought that they have will not come into the obedience of a fearful God. Their thoughts will be devoid of what is morally right as opposed to thoughts that are careful to please Him. A holy reverence for God causes you to be fearful of offending Him in anything. Children are apt to do foolish things. It is a good thing to never call a child a fool, but it is wise to *know* that they will do foolish things. Foolishness should be taught against for it ignores wisdom. Wisdom, the proper application of gained knowledge, must be taught, too.

The more wisdom that a youth obtains, the more they will fear God as they grow to respect and honor His ways, because wisdom is the mind of God.

➤ Expect Obedience

In training up a child to live in a manner that represents the Kingdom of God, the goal is to help the child conform to the biblical education and the spiritual formation you oversee. Pleasing to the heart of God is a mother who attends to His precepts, and gives that Word to their child for instruction. "Honor your father and your mother" is the fifth commandment and an admonishment in **Ephesians 6:2**. The first step is for children to hear the instructions of their parents. Children who take notice of and pay attention to biblically sound wisdom, insight, and revelation from their mother are blessed with seed sown into their development that will order their steps.

The instruction of God says, "My son, hear the instruction of your father; reject not nor forsake the teaching of your mother" (Proverbs 1:8). [AMPC] God puts an emphasis on *instruction* and *teaching*, and it is from these two actions that a child's obedience should come. Mothers should insist on obedience. Your sons and daughters should obey you because:

- ➤ It is the right thing to do;
- ➤ God, through His Word, commands it; and
- ➤ The teachings of Jesus (The Gospel) would have children to obey their parents.

When children are trained in the fear and admonition of the Lord it impacts their vision of God. A child who has a proper vision of God will hold their parents in high regard, and even see their parents as "God's representative on earth." A mother working to instill a high regard for God creates a high regard for herself. On the other hand, if a child is disobedient to a parent they are indirectly being taught to be disobedient to God.

Dr. Bryan Chapell says, "If we love our children too much to require them to do what is right, then we have not really loved them enough."

➤ **Model with Integrity**

Mothers should model with integrity which is simply living what you say; living what you profess;, and living what you want your child to do. It is highly important to be a model for your child, so they can catch the essence of Godly living. Be a model, and when you miss the mark, it is okay. Tell your child, that you missed it. Come home and tell your husband in front of the child, "You know I really missed it. I did this or that, and I apologize." Live with what you say. One thing to know, mom, is that their eyes are always on you. When you don't think they're looking, when you don't think they're hearing, they are. Your children look to see how you respond. Your response teaches them how to respond. All your responses will not be perfect, but let that be your aim; and again, when you miss it, apologize sincerely and go on with your day.

Model with integrity. Always model what you want. If you're not the best model, get them involved with somebody who is. That's the power of good provisional relationships in your lives, especially when they possess a skill set that you do not have. Exposure can be key in making your child aware of an example that may be better than yours. Be careful, however, to explain to your son or daughter that while you haven't reached a particular level, what you are presenting to them is what you are working towards in your own life. Let them see your efforts and your accomplishments.

God makes it clear that availability to your children is of the utmost importance. You are going to become a greater servant to your child by giving them greater access to you. And through you and by you, they are going to have more access to God. They may *think* that they are, but in reality, they are not ready to navigate this world by themselves, for this world is too much for them right now. Too many children fail because they have never gained the wisdom to navigate this world in Christ. They have to learn to navigate the world and a mother's love is a sure agent to help them do that.

Be consistently available to your child. Accompany them. Be with them through the early development of their life (from birth to college especially). It's going to be wonderful when they come back at 30 with fruit, and not a request for a loan. Declare that you are going to see from their life the fruit of Christ, because you have lived with them.

15

Next Level Mothering

he fact that God gave you your children means that they are a reward. Because they are a reward, they should be handled as a reward and not as a project. Kids are not projects. Mom, you are not just trying to rush through life to get them out of the house or on their own. Like an architect, you are building them as an extension of the hand of God and forming Christ inside of them. I hope that by now you see your child as an arrow that has to be shot into this present generation and beyond. You should want them to go as far as they can go; but you also want to aim them accurately and strategically, so that they are positioned to enter into whatever they were designed by God to go into.

To every mother who reads these pages, do know that I value you tremendously! Remember, mothers, you share in God's image. God has included you in His agenda to manifest Himself in the earth by placing His qualities inside of you. Beyond the gift of reproduction to replenish the population, I remind you that you have the influence to shape your child's life so that the culture of nations can be impacted.

If you just look at the culture of most nations today, you'll see that they are ill-equipped to become what was initially envisioned and declared about them. I ask you, "Will you train a child up who will simply maintain the status quo or will you train up children who will bring blessings to any society as well as transformation?" For your child to bring transformation into a culture, you will be required to cultivate God and His Kingdom inside your child above any other thing that you administer in their lives. I know there are dreams and desires that you may have for your child that may not align themselves with things I have articulated in this writing; and I know that there are many opportunities that "would lead to their fame or greatness."

Please, hear me by the Spirit, for what I *don't* want you to do is to be consumed with your child becoming rich, famous, and influential in ways that are outside of the Kingdom of God and its principles. That should never be a parent's aim. You cannot live through your child and say, "Well I hope they have all that I never had." From God's perspective, gain that lasts will never come by the ways of humanism or ideologies that are centered in what is most socially acceptable. Again, true progress means the Kingdom of God is the most important thing that you administer in their lives.

Indoctrinating your child into the ways of God is like getting medicine into them. You have to be that adamant and that focused to get the medicine of the Kingdom into your child. So again, it moves you into a place where you and your husband, for those of you who are married, really work together to get the Kingdom into your child's life. If you are living in a shared custody situation where you have the kids sometimes and their father has them at other times, you have to work together to integrate the Kingdom of God somehow into that structure.

Once your kids leaves your home, you cannot control the environment that they may enter. But the time you put in upfront, before they encounter an environment that may not honor the Kingdom of God, must be intentional, consistent, and well thought out in order to preserve the seeds you have sown. The people and places they encounter that are the opposite of what you teach can be withstood, but I think that it will require *Mothering at the Next Level.*

Mothering at the Next Level will assist you in cultivating the reward (your child) God has given you. **First Samuel 2:35** says *...and I will raise up for Myself a faithful priest who shall do according to what is in My heart and my mind.* [AMPC]

What would it feel like if God told you that He has taken your child, and will raise them up as a faithful priest? What happens when God whispers that to you about your boy or girl, and you labor with Him? The result: your child will become a faithful priest unto God! That's where we are headed in this section. Let's go ahead and declare that you are training up a priest. *And I will build him a sure house that he shall walk before My anointed forever,* saith the Lord.

Matthew 6:33 says, *But seek first the kingdom of God and His righteousness (His way of doing and being right) and then all these things taken together will be given you besides.* [AMPC]

God is saying that all these things that you need will be given unto you because you have stewarded your children and grandchildren the right way. Dennis Peacocke, one of my mentors, is phenomenal in his understanding of Kingdom stewardship. As an apostolic leader his capacity for strategic thinking continues to be a conduit for transforming nations. Let me form this contextually. Understand that your child is a resource from God and you are stewarding them.

I want to give you some practical stewarding principles that I believe are going to cause your child to move in such a manifested consecration unto God that it would be obvious to all who encounter them that they have been set aside for God because of what's coming out of their lives (which is the result of what you are putting into their lives.)

➤ 16

You are the church

Think on this: you are the church. According to scripture, you are the temple of the Holy Spirit (**1 Corinthians 6:19**). The things that happen in your local church should be the things that come out of you daily. The church is the physical building, you are the spiritual building. As you live your life, you should live it with the power and glory that come out of the formal church worship gathering. I like to reference it as such:

> ➤ **Your life should be a mobile worship gathering**.

And what comes out of your life should be what goes on in the worship center you attend with other believers. So let us look at things that I think will assist you in this journey. As a parent, you should be the one to lead your child to Christ. I believe that when it is possible, the salvation experience should be administered by a child's parent. (**Romans 10:9,10**).

Mothers, I believe that your aim is to ensure that your child is saved and that Jesus is the Lord of their life and that they understand that. Kevin Haag, a contemporary Christian educator, has a great online resource for that application at **new-testament-christian.com**.

I am not opposed to a child giving their life to Christ through church, a summer camp, a youth worker, or other valid avenues. However if you are in tune with your child and are spending time to train them up in the things of God, mom, you will know when the timing is right to offer the Good News of Christ to your child, but only if they understand the commitment they're making.

All of the scriptures in Romans 3:10-18 (also known as the Romans Road to Salvation) should be fully understood at the time of your child's salvation, and then be revisited periodically as your son or daughter matriculates through their early life. Furthermore, they should know what salvation is; that it's more than just saying "I am saved;" and that it is being able to communicate what salvation is and lead others through the Romans Road scriptures.

➢ Dedicate your children to God

It is good for your child to know that they have been dedicated to the Creator of the universe and the Creator of their life.

- -In the first chapter of First Samuel Hannah presents her son, Samuel, to the Lord.
- -In Luke 2:22 we read that Mary and Joseph brought their baby Jesus to the temple in Jerusalem in order to present Him before the Lord.

Note: A child can be dedicated at anytime, anywhere, but I believe it is prudent to bring them to the house of the Lord in keeping with Jesus' dedication. It is good that at every new stage a child enters there be some form of rededication subsequent to the original dedication.

Suggested Times of Dedication

Starting Nursery or Kindergarten

Starting Elementary School

Turning 13 Years of Age (See Meaning For The Jewish Bat and Bar Mitzvah)

Starting Middle School

Starting High School

Starting College

Entering Into Extracurricular Activities

Entering College

Graduating College

Entering Post College

Entering Profession

Be diligent to rededicate them to God because after their initial dedication they may fall away from the faith in some areas of their life. It is important for them to know they can go boldly back to God in spite of how far they have drifted from His ways. This assurance will impact their perspective on the Savior. God will never get tired of you presenting your child at His feet as often as you need to.

➢ Express The Love Of God

Communicating love should never ever stop. God is love and His love is a biblical truth (**1 John 4:8**). Never stop showing love. Do what love does. I often tell my children that I love them and then I add to it that, "God loves you, too." When you release a declaration of the love of God to your child they may not necessarily respond to you, but they will respond to the One who made them. It really communicates a sense of belonging, acceptance, and hope. It is reassuring to know that the God of all has seen fit to touch the heart of someone who in turn reaches out to them and relays God's heart.

To be thought of by God is almost unfathomable for adults and children alike, but it is real and this truth must be expressed to everyone. Always communicate that to your children, and that they are loved by *you*. Look for opportunities to express and demonstrate this powerful emotion.

➤ 17

Form love in your child

elp your child to become a loving child. Teach them what love is and what love does. Make it known to them through the examples of how Jesus lived --Matthew, Mark, Luke, and John. Discover it in how Apostle Paul taught the Christian church to live together in love from the book of Romans to the book of Jude. His writings were sent to people to show them how to live in Christ, in His love toward one another. Children need to know why it is important to live life loving all people. No one accepts all of anyone's ways, but we should love all people, even if we disagree with what they do or what they stand for.

Teach them to express love in simple ways. For example, as your child outgrows their clothing, don't sell them; instead donate them. Take the clothes along with your son or daughter to the Goodwill or Salvation Army. Let them be the ones to hand the donations to the attendant. An exercise like this teaches them how to express love and care for other people. Teach your child to love other people and always to discover and honor the "least of those"--the person who seems to be left out and left behind. Teach your child to go to that person, serve them, or offer something to them that is tangible or emotional. It is a good thing for a child to know how to give of themselves.

➢ **Communicate the value of loving.**

Love should be held in high esteem by all people. It is centered first in loving God and then loving other people. Children need to know that Love is a virtue that is higher than all other virtues. When it is incorporated in their lives they love God, others, and themselves in ways that are proper and admirable.

Love is invaluable. What it can cause for the good in any situation is beyond what most could ever imagine. Our world is truly devoid of God's love, but if you are able, and I believe you are, you can heighten its importance and awareness in your child's life. And if you do, he or she will ascend to heights in the culture that allow them to connect with and influence most of the world's population.

Love has as its root the following: **Luke 10:27**

And he replied, You must love the Lord your God with all your heart and with all your soul and with all your strength and with all your mind; and your neighbor as yourself. [AMPC]

From the application above, love in Christ, can be realized. One is then enabled to live in pursuit of **1 Corinthians 13:4-8** which guides us and serves as our goal in loving others. It says, *4 Love endures long and is patient and kind; love never is envious nor boils over with jealousy, is not boastful or vainglorious, does not display itself haughtily.*

5 It is not conceited (arrogant and inflated with pride);

it is not rude (unmannerly) and does not act unbecomingly. Love (God's love in us) does not insist on its own rights or its own way, for it is not self-seeking; it is not touchy or fretful or resentful; it takes no account of the evil done to it [it pays no attention to a suffered wrong].

6 It does not rejoice at injustice and unrighteousness, but rejoices when right and truth prevail.

7 Love bears up under anything and everything that comes, is ever ready to believe the best of every person, its hopes are fadeless under all circumstances, and it endures everything [without weakening].

8 Love never fails [never fades out or becomes obsolete or comes to an end]. As for prophecy ([a]the gift of interpreting the divine will and purpose), it will be fulfilled and pass away; as for tongues, they will be destroyed and cease; as for knowledge, it will pass away [it will lose its value and be superseded by truth]. [AMPC]

➤ 18

Teach your child how to pray

hile they may not be able to see prayer as dialogue with God, that's exactly what it is. A dialogue with God is the highest form of communication that a person can have. How to pray was the only recorded thing that the disciples who walked with Jesus ever asked Him to teach them to do.

Luke 11:1 *Then He was praying in a certain place; and when He stopped, one of His disciples said to Him, Lord,* **teach us to pray***, [just] as John taught his disciples.* [AMPC]

Children should not be stuck all of their lives at "Now I lay me down to sleep," or "Lord, we thank you for this food." These prayers are fine at the toddler stage, but they will not bring personal, corporate, or global change. Your focus is to train your child in prayers that will one day move heaven. I encourage parents to teach their children to pray:

- By praying with them
- By teaching them how to pray alone
- By teaching them to pray for others

Heaven possesses all that we could ever need. Jesus understood this and encouraged the disciples to pray that what was in Heaven--God's throne room of unlimited resources--would manifest on earth and meet needs (as established by God and His will) according to His riches in glory.

Luke 11:2 reveals

2 And He said to them, When you pray, say: Our Father Who is in heaven, hallowed be Your name, **Your kingdom come.** *Your will be done [held holy and revered]* **on earth as it is in heaven.** [AMPC]

It is only the Kingdom of God that will change this world we live in and when we pray for His Kingdom to come and for His will on earth to be like things are in heaven, the world experiences change. The disciples prayed like this, with understanding, but most people do not. The Lord's Prayer serves as a guide for prayer and is segmented as follows: It is a set of decrees and declarations Jesus taught the disciples which obviously have the power and authority to bring the resources and ways of heaven into the earth, even our lives.

> **Matthew 6:9-13**

✓ *Our Father Who is in heaven, hallowed (kept holy) be Your name.*

It is here that our Father God, who is in heaven should be approached in reverence, which is a healthy fear because of His greatness. Teach your child the names of God, for they all declare many of His attributes.

To hallow His name is to ascribe to it worth and value. It is at this place in prayer that honor (great respect, high rank and position) to God are expressed.

✓ *Your kingdom come, Your will be done on earth as it is in heaven.*

The greatest, most meaningful and impactful kingdom is the Kingdom of God. The greatest will to be fulfilled on earth is the will (desires and purposes) of God. This place in prayer is where you can teach your children to ask or decree that God's Kingdom and His will shall come into all things.

✓ *Give us this day our daily bread.*

God meets all of our needs according to His riches in glory. As King in this Kingdom, He is responsible for our provision. In love, honor, and respect we can implore Him to give us the things that He, in His omniscience, knows that we need. All things are not needs; some are wants, and in prayer you learn the difference by how God answers your requests. He is obligated to meet needs, not wants.

✓ *And forgive us our debts, as we also have forgiven ([a]left, remitted, and let go of the debts, and have [b]given up resentment against) our debtors.*

Asking for forgiveness is pleasing to God. Children should know that it is quite easy to sin, but to ask for forgiveness cleanses us from that sin. When sin is committed, encourage them to repent. Explain that repenting means that they are to turn away from their particular wrongdoing and go in the opposite direction in how they think and respond to the temptation that caused them to sin. Help them to recount their sins daily and ask for forgiveness through their repentance.

The greatest demonstration of this in the Bible is Psalm 52 when David goes to the Lord in authentic repentance and receives forgiveness for his wrongdoing. Note that authentic repentance is key. The Lord is always faithful and just to cleanse us from all unrighteousness (**1 John 1:9**). In communicating how forgiveness releases us from our sins, tell them that it is the will of God that they forgive anyone who has done wrong to them. If you do not forgive others for sinning against you, God will not forgive you.

Matthew 6:14-15

But if you do forgive people of their trespasses(their reckless and willful sins, leaving them, letting them go, and giving up resentment), your heavenly Father will also forgive you. But if you do not forgive others their trespasses (their reckless and willful sins, leaving them, letting them go, and give up resentment) neither will your heavenly Father forgive you your trespasses. [AMPC]

And if your child asks how often we should forgive someone, explain this to them.

Matthew 18:21-22

Then Peter came up to Him and said, Lord, how many times may my brother sin against me and I forgive him and let it go? (As many as) up to seven times? [AMPC]

Jesus answered him. I tell you, not up to seven times, but 70 times seven! Help your boy or girl to understand that forgiving someone actually is treating that person the way God treats you. Once we experience God's forgiveness, we should treat others the same way.

Ephesians 4:32

And become useful and helpful to one another, tenderhearted (compassionate, understanding, loving-hearted), forgiving one another (readily and freely), as God in Christ forgave you. [AMPC]

✓ *And lead (bring) us not into temptation, but deliver us from the evil one.*

It is good to know that God never tempts us.

James 1:13 tells us to *Let no one say when he is tempted, I am tempted from God; for God is incapable of being tempted by (what is) evil and He Himself tempts no one.*[AMPC]

Therefore, God is willing to lead us NOT into temptation if we respond to His leading us away from sinful things. How you explain who the "evil one" is should be done with wisdom. If your child is not aware of the devil, satan, then teach him from the perspective of good and evil.

> ➤ **God is the Good Person. Satan is the evil one.**

We want to be delivered (set free or saved) from the things the evil one does which cause us to be disobedient to God and can even create pain in our lives. We want to pursue the Good One because it makes us and our lives better. Your child needs to know they can ask God to lead them away from temptation, and deliver them from the evil one and his sinful ways.

Again it is wise to handle this matter with much prayer. The objective is not to cause the child to become afraid of the devil, but to have a good strong relationship with Jesus, and let no evil tempt them to dishonor God. This defeats evil.

✓ *For Yours is the kingdom and the power and the glory forever. Amen.*

Here we express confidence in God through all that has been lifted to Him in prayer. And here the Kingdom, the Power, and the Glory are recognized as His own. He is the Overseer of His Kingdom. He has the power or ability to do all things, and His Glory is eternal. The economy of God holds in it everything that is needed to build and manifest fruit in the life of a child. There is nothing greater than discovering ways and means by which a child can grow and fulfill their potential. The following will assist you further in laying and maintaining foundations that will awaken purpose and destiny in your children.

When you expose your child to what is spiritually correct and accurate, and it helps them to gain understanding, it is pleasing to the Lord. One accepts all of anyone's ways, but we should love all people, even if we disagree with what they do or what they stand for.

➤ 19

Spirit Living

Make children knowledgeable of:

Holy Spirit and the Baptism of the Holy Spirit

Christian author, Mary Fairchild speaks of Him as such, "The Holy Spirit is the third Person of the Trinity. The Trinity expresses the belief that God is one being made up of three distinct persons who exist in co-equal and co-eternal communion as the Father, Son, and Holy Spirit. However, without a personal name like God the Father or His son Jesus Christ, Holy Spirit seems distant to many, yet he dwells inside every true believer and is a constant companion in the walk of faith."

Jesus, in the book of **Acts 1:8** says to His disciples before his departure to Heaven:

8 But you shall receive power (ability, efficiency, and might) when the Holy Spirit has come upon you, and you shall be My witnesses in Jerusalem and all Judea and Samaria and to the ends (the very bounds) of the earth. [AMPC]

The Holy Spirit should become the constant companion of your child. He is not Someone to be recognized in church only; but He is here to lead, guide, instruct, and direct your children through the daily affairs of their lives.

In **Acts 2:1-4** we see the writings of Luke as he describes what Jesus said they would receive in Acts 1:8.

1 And when the day of Pentecost had fully come, they were all assembled together in one place,2 When suddenly there came a sound from heaven like the rushing of a violent tempest blast, and it filled the whole house in which they were sitting. 3 And there appeared to them tongues resembling fire, which were separated and distributed and

which settled on each one of them. ⁴ And they were all filled
(diffused throughout their souls) with the Holy Spirit and
began to speak in other (different, foreign) languages
(tongues), as the Spirit [ᵃ]kept giving them clear and loud
expression [in each tongue in appropriate words]. [AMPC]

It is here that the 120 believers in the Upper Room
were baptized into the Holy Spirit by Jesus. I think many
fear Holy Spirit because He entered the Upper Room in a
way that probably looked like and felt like an explosive,
blockbuster Hollywood movie. There is nothing
destructive about Him, but when we recall that Jesus said
He would come as a power source, then it is
understandable that His entrance, carrying all the power
of God into a small room, would certainly be as a mighty-
rushing wind.

For your children to live a life above the hardships
and difficulties that they will face; and needing the
wisdom of God to overcome all adversarial contention,
Holy Spirit is necessary as the most important helper who

will aid them in overcoming all of the onslaughts of evil that are so prevalent in our society. He is a Gift from God to your child. I encourage you to unwrap Him.

➤ 20

Teaching salvation and the Kingdom and culture of God

M Teach your child how to share the Good News of Jesus Christ. It is good that your child knows how to share the greatest message of our time with others. The Romans Road is a navigational system for you to teach your child that they may follow it in leading people into a relationship with Jesus. {Romans 3:10-18, Romans 3:23, Romans 5:8, Romans 6:23, Romans 10:9-10, Romans 10:13.}

That is the navigational system to salvation. When a child learns this, they are then able to administer the greatest miracle that there is, and that is a person moving from a life of hopelessness into new life that can only be found in Jesus. Travel this road with your child and declare that eternal fruit will come from it.

I Apologetically challenge my oldest son because I know he's in college, so he's exposed to a lot of anti-Christian beliefs. And so I'm constantly challenging him Apologetically to see if he can defend the faith. To see if he can he stand when he's in a world where people are coming against the things of God. My aim is to sharpen his spiritual acumen, his witness of Jesus; who He is and what He stands for. Can he reason with others? I realize that the more he exercises his spiritual muscles, the surer he'll feel in his walk with God, which should increase his confidence when leading other people into the knowledge of the God of the Bible.

If they have not already done so, your child will come to you and share all types of mindsets and attitudes that people have, especially as they get into high school and then college. It is vital that you sharpen your biblical worldview to speak to that while seeding the Kingdom into their spirit. Your children will come home repeating what other kids are saying and it is imperative that you form in them counter stances that support the Kingdom of God. What are you doing to counter these advances? I assure you that your children are well able to absorb the teachings of the Kingdom of God.

Being open and sensitive to their lives, and the questions and things that are going on with them; and having biblical responses serves to train and equip them to be great witnesses for Jesus. You are then training them to have an active walk with God.

➤ Fasting

Fasting is abstaining from food. I encourage fasting that is under the supervision of a parent or guardian. At least once a week your child should abstain from food or something else; but I only recommend it for teenagers and adults. At least once a week I would encourage a voluntary fast. I have a friend in ministry who fasted as a youth, and he attributes a measure of his significance in and to the body of Christ to learning to fast as a child.

Fasting Disclaimer:

Neither Apostle Terrell Murphy, nor Life Center International, or any entities of Life Center International will be held responsible for any adverse physical reactions to a fast.

➢ **Prophesying**

Help your child to understand what it is to prophesy. To prophesy is to decree the Word of God. Any Word of God that is decreed is prophesying. Speaking the Word of God is far greater than speaking the words of the majority of hip hop artists, movie stars, and most leaders in the nations of the world. I am not speaking of the traditional mindset of preaching *per se*; but being able at given times to say what God has said in His Word.

The places that your children go are filled with anti-Christ verbiage and philosophies. When they can share the Word of God with a young friend about a behavior, attitude, or situation that they may be facing, they can change that friend's life. God's Word has something to say about drug use, sex before marriage, riotous living, and honoring parents—all matters that children discuss and encounter daily.

Then there's prophecy relative to speaking of forthcoming events. This is a gift that is given by Holy Spirit and should be developed in your child by individuals in your church who train prophets. If your church tells you that these gifts have stopped, then I would encourage you to consult a Spirit-filled church that believes in the gifts of the Spirit (1 Corinthians 12: 1-11). If your child is prophesying and someone says that those gifts stopped with the early church then how can your child be doing it? Spiritual gifts will be with us until the return of Christ. Just food for thought.

➤ Laying on of Hands

The laying on of hands is a biblical action; however it is not a biblical mandate. While not obligatory, it was a practice of Jesus. The laying on of hands sets your child apart as it signifies the imparting of spiritual blessings, authority, and power. In the Old Testament a blessing was often conferred in this way (Jacob –Genesis 48:13-20). I believe it is a good practice to lay hands upon your child, and empower them to excel by the impartation of Godly attributes and virtues that can be passed through this biblical action.

➤ Servitude

*S*ervitude is an avenue to greatness. To attend to another person, especially those from whom you cannot benefit is noble. Most children of this generation have been served and served well. Parents have gone to incredible lengths to take care of the needs of their children. While I understand this approach, if it is not balanced by cultivating a mindset in a child that giving is better than receiving, and that serving is greater than being served, your son or daughter will think that the world revolves around them. Serving should begin at home as the members of a family live from the perspective that each is worthy of being attended to as often as it can be done. Serve, Mom.

When a culture of servitude is nurtured at home, it overflows from your children into society. The population of this world benefits from people who serve it. Enlighten your children about the importance, value, and benefits of serving each other, the community, and the nations. There are limitless opportunities for serving in your home and community.

Cultivating and activating a spirit of servitude in your child will help as they come into your place of worship. A lot of behavior that children develop at home and in society works against the Kingdom of God. Not being a servant is one of those. The Kingdom of God is advanced by people who see the importance of serving the church and its initiatives inside and outside of the church for the sake of Jesus Christ. It is a good thing to teach how Jesus served the entire world; how He willingly laid down His life in order to serve every person who accepts His sacrifice, that they might receive eternal life in heaven. He still serves and cares for the world today.

Let your children see what it looks like to serve from your example. Take them somewhere and let them serve in a soup kitchen; let them be a part of an outreach ministry. Let them step out of their comfort zone and do things that stretch them. Challenge them with a chance to serve. These things are very important because you are preparing children to advance the Kingdom of God; and it is advanced by serving Jesus and the people He loves.

Servitude is a doorway into the next level of life. It manifests favor, increase, and promotion. It should never be done out of selfish ambition to get ahead. Rather, service should be offered because we honor and respect others; and because we are mature enough and secure enough to treat them and value them more highly than ourselves.

Jesus was God in flesh, and yet through all the signs, wonders, and miracles He performed, He still took off His robe, kneeled down, and washed the feet of His disciples. He never stopped serving even unto His death on the cross, for even then He was serving humanity. That's your child's model. That's their answer to "why they should serve." Train and equip them to serve all the days of their lives.

➢ **Wisdom**

Train your children in wisdom. Children have a way of doing what is stupid and dumb and ignorant and nonsensical. Discover personally, then pass to them the answers to these questions.

- What is wisdom?

- Why is wisdom necessary?

- How do children get wisdom?

● What do they do with wisdom?

● What can wisdom create for and from their life?

Help them to understand that a reverent fear of God is the beginning of wisdom. Teach them to fear God by following what He says and does. That's the beginning of wisdom. The more they follow God's ways, the more wisdom they will receive.

➢ **The Kingdom of God**

The Kingdom of God is the rule and reign of God in all of the earth, even the universe. It is the rule over our hearts and lives through submission to God. Help your child to understand the Kingdom of God in what is written above. It is beneficial to a child to know that the greatest quality of life is found in God's Kingdom. You will be amazed at the things your child can tell you about in other kingdoms.

Sometimes my boys are going back and forth, and their mom will say something like, "I can't believe that y'all know that much about that..."(or whatever the subject is). It is because they are so tapped into social networking and all of the information channels that are available to them. And children talk about a gamut of things. Well, why not the Kingdom? They are going to talk about what they are exposed to. Your kids will talk about what they know.

Do this: Find things that help them to know the Kingdom. Remember, they talk about what they know. You are their teacher, and a good one at that; and you are their leader. Learn of the Kingdom and explore ways to inspire your children to think about God and His Kingdom. I declare to you that if you seek the ingenuity, creativity, and wisdom to do it, God will respond and release them to you.

➢ Gifts of the Spirit

A benefit and possession of those who believe in and follow Jesus are spiritual gifts. Spiritual gifts are given to God's people by the Holy Spirit for the "common good," or in the best interest of all those who are in the Body of Christ and even outside of the Body of Christ. (1 Corinthians 12:11)

Spiritual gifts are not natural gifts. Natural gifts and talents are the results of genetics or surroundings; they may also be bestowed upon someone because God endowed the person with them. Spiritual gifts are given *only* to believers, those who confess Jesus as their Lord and Savior. It is through a personal relationship with Him that the avenue into spiritual gifts opens.

Mother, I am hopeful that your child will become a believer or is a believer. Discovering and cultivating their spiritual gifts is a means by which your child, as a believer, can most effectively contribute to the Body of Christ. In the New Testament we read of the Apostles operating in their gifts, but we also read of individuals like Phillip and Ananias who ministered their spiritual gifts, and brought significant change for the upbuilding of the church and people outside of the church as well.

But earnestly desire and zealously cultivate the greatest and best gifts and graces (the higher gifts and the choicest graces). (**1 Corinthians 12:31**) [AMPC]

➤ **The Fruit of the Spirit**

Galatians 5:22-23 tells us, *But the fruit of the [Holy] Spirit [the work which His presence within accomplishes] is love, joy (gladness), peace, patience (an even temper, forbearance), kindness, goodness (benevolence), faithfulness, 23 Gentleness (meekness, humility), self-control (self-restraint,). Against such things there is no law that can bring a charge].* [AMPC]

The fruit of the Holy Spirit is the result of salvation. Jesus wants your children to receive salvation so that they can take hold of the greater experience of living in Jesus. The greater experience is the workings of Holy Spirit, of whom Jesus said He would come in power. Salvation, spiritual gifts, the fruit of the Spirit, as well the baptism of the Holy Spirit are all workings of Holy Spirit which have been set aside for believers so that we can live victoriously.

Wow! What a loving God to set all this up for us; and it is for your children, too--not when they get to be adults, but at the time of salvation. I encourage you to pray to the Lord for them to receive salvation when they are old enough to understand what Jesus did for them on the cross. The fruit of the Spirit is in direct contrast with the sinful nature (Galatians 5:19-21).

Your child will always battle with temptations of their flesh (their sinful nature), but as you help them to identify what the fruit of the Spirit is and how they can and should pursue those qualities instead of the works of their sinful nature, they will have the wonderful image of Jesus formed in them in a loving way by Holy Spirit.

➢ Scripture Memorization

Memorization is one of the most effective means of engaging scripture. In leading your children to understand, grasp, and apply the Word of God, teaching them to ponder a scripture over and over is a great way for them to memorize a particular passage and gain spiritual insight.

Memorization is not new to your children. They have memorized things all the days of their kindergarten, elementary, middle, and high school matriculation. This gives you the advantage in assisting them with scripture memorization. It is just helping them to do what they have been doing for many years. The most challenging part of it, however, may be for them to realize that it is good to memorize the Word of God, even more than the lyrics of their favorite song.

So why is the Word of God worth memorizing? It is because its greatest benefit is that the Word is life-giving spirit. His spoken words that are heard and kept (practiced, obeyed, held true), are spirit, and impart the life of God to the hearer. Only words that are spoken by God will give life. The Word of God brings an individual life. This is spiritual life, a type of life that is essential for the continued existence of something. In this case, that "something" is your child. Your child needs what is essential for their productive existence. See, the Word of God is actually God Himself! For He is the Word (**John 1:1**). In the Word of God is life, His life. He is in His Word.

When your child memorizes the Word of God which comes about by mulling over that Word, just as they do rap lyrics, that Word is sown into them; and the instructions, warnings, conclusions, and directions of that Word come alive in relation to what your child is encountering--especially when he or she is being tempted. When the Word is recalled, the Spirit of God and the life that is in that Word awaken your child to the truth of that Word and assist them in responding to what they have been meditating on. When they act on what they have meditated on, success comes forth and the spirit and life of Christ are enriched in them.

Your child should memorize by subject matters, because a productive life requires us to respond properly to the many subject matters that your children will engage all of their lives. Here's an exercise you can do with your child: List as many subject matters as you can think of, which are relevant to the life of a child—laziness, honoring parents, attending school, being responsible, etc.

Now find what scripture says about each subject matter, and begin to assist your child in memorizing those scriptures. They will experience the Word (God) being very near to them as they become alive to the Word by His Spirit.

It is good to help your child memorize shorter scriptures and scriptures that can help someone when spoken to them "off the cuff," meaning without preparation. Scriptures that comfort, encourage, and give hope are a good place to start as well. In the section where I addressed witnessing, scriptures that help someone become a Christian would apply here. Help your child to become excited about memorizing God's Word. The benefits of this discipline will be eternally rewarding.

➢ Church Membership

Church membership is very important. Romans 12: 5 says that, *So we, numerous as we are, are one body in Christ (the Messiah) and individually we are parts one of another (mutually dependent on one another).* What Apostle Paul was communicating was that every believer is a member of the universal church and in addition, each believer should be a part of a church in the local community.

Children need to understand that church membership is required by God so that we all are in a place where God has planted us. As you are training your child up to be pleasing to God, do convey to them that God delights in your being in a local church and there are congregational blessings and favor that come from being a member of a church.

I will set my dwelling (Tabernacle) in and among you, and my soul shall not despise or reject or separate itself from you. And I will walk in and with and among you and will be your God, and you shall be My people. (**Leviticus 26:11-12**) [AMPC]

Your child will benefit greatly throughout their lives when they grasp the importance of being planted by God to serve in a local church in order to bring to pass the vision God has for their church.

➢ **Understanding Vision**

Teach children that there is a God-ordered vision that He has for the church to which they are joined. Practically applying the vision of a ministry house is the responsibility of the members and it comes to pass when there is participation by each one according to what each one supplies. In the Book of Joshua, it was he who led the children of Israel into the Promised Land, but it was not the parents he was leading; it was the children and grandchildren of those adults who would be the ones who moved the body forward. There was no going out to find substitute children to complete the vision; it was the offspring who arrived at and went into the better place that God had ordained.

The younger generations must keep the local church going. I think that deserves a conversation at your dinner table periodically. Just as your children have to keep your family advancing and journeying toward significance, the spiritual family that they are a part of should benefit from the same zeal, focus, and commitment to destiny!

Mothers, you can sit with your children and talk about their role in advancing and preserving the ministry of your local church. And furthermore, with purposefulness and intentionality, communicate to them that as Christians, it is required of us to serve the vision of the place where we worship.

➤ Giving

Benevolence and charity are staples in the Christian life.

Acts 20:35 declares that, *In everything I have pointed out to you [by example] that, by working diligently in this manner, we ought to assist the weak, being mindful of the words of the Lord Jesus, how He Himself said, it is more blessed (makes one happier and more envied) to give than receive.*

As stated earlier, going to Goodwill and to the Salvation Army are important; and even going to neighbors or friends who have needs, is a great way to cultivate a heart for giving in your children. The softer the heart and the more understanding they have of giving, the easier it will be when they reach the place of seeding finances into God's Kingdom. Begin at the principle that "Everything belongs to God," and in His kindness, He only asks for a small portion to be returned back to Him via tithes, which is 10 percent of our gross earnings; and in offerings, which is as an act of faith, we prayerfully give a meaningful amount of money. Tithing was established before the laws which were given by God to the Israelites at an amount of 10 percent. The tithe is an obligation to give. The offering is an opportunity to give, and the best practice is to teach him or her to pray, and ask God what should they give as an offering, and to trust that He will lead them.

I believe that one of the worst things that you or any other mother could do would be to put no emphasis on benevolence, charity, tithes, or offerings with your child. To ignore these proven means of financial prosperity is to set up an subconscious barrier between your child and the blessings of God which will play itself out in their lives as they confront the choice to give or not to give to God.

The earlier they start to give–materially or financially--the more pleasing to God and the more prosperous in their affairs they will be.

➤ Honoring Spiritual Leadership

It is good to give honor where honor is due. Mothers, honor is an attribute that will release favor to your child.

Now also we beseech you brethren, get to know those who labor among you and [recognize them for what they are, acknowledge and appreciate and respect them all]-your leaders who are over you in the Lord and those who warn and kindly reprove and exhort you. And hold them in very high and most affectionate esteem in [intelligent and sympathetic] appreciation of their work. Be at peace among yourselves. (**1 Thessalonians 5:12-13**) [AMPC]

Teach them early how to appropriately honor their spiritual leadership.

➤ 21

God's new thing

"Behold, I am doing a new thing! Now it springs forth; do you not perceive and know it and will you not give heed to it? I will even make a way in the wilderness and rivers in the desert."(**Isaiah 43:19**) (AMPC)

Mother, God has given you a responsibility, and while it is the same one that your mom had, it is quite different in how it must come to pass. This dispensation of time in which you are training your child has challenges that will require the aid of God like no other generation has needed Him ever before. Your children need to do more than just get by or survive.

They need to do more than just exist and blend in with the crowd, maintaining the status quo which is heading toward futility. They need to be more than the kid down the street, the athlete, the academic, or the beauty queen. I applaud any accomplishment of any child, but what I am passionate about is a child moving beyond what the natural eye can see into being what was conceived in the spirit realm.

Children must take hold of their destiny--their anointed destination. Their destination was determined by God, and not the nations. It was not determined by their abilities nor even their wonderful mothers. What they possess is a plan and a purpose inside of them that God planted there. You were set apart by God for the children that are in your care. No one can fulfill the role that you were handpicked by God to play in their lives. God trusts you and that is why you are stewarding His creation for Him. The Lord would have you to return to the ancient path.

The ancient path is the way He established for you to be successful in training up your child--son, daughter, niece, nephew, grandson, granddaughter, foster child, or the one who is yet unborn who will come into your life and change it for the good forever--in the way that He marked out ages ago. One of my prayers is that you would find yourselves in a place where you consciously begin to carve out time to do what you have read. To say you do not have time, well, I have to say to you, "That is unacceptable!" Your son or daughter is a heritage and a gift from God. They have been released from God to *you*!

Therefore, I decree and declare that God's good work in every child whose mom is reading and applying this manual to their child-rearing, training, and equipping, will manifest, and that all God ever spoke concerning you, and all He designed you for will come to pass!

Grace Grace, Mothers!

➤ 22

Consecration: A prayer for the arrow in your hand

Heavenly Father I am grateful to You for placing this arrow in my hand .I submit them to You by name. (Name each child in your care). The Bible declares, and I believe, that my child is a heritage from the Lord, the fruit of the womb and a reward--all of which I am truly grateful for. It also declares that "...as arrows in the hand of a warrior, so are the children of one's youth." Therefore, I realize that You consecrated my offspring before they were even formed in my womb. I am confident in You and look to You for the enhancement of what You have ordained for me to mother. I stand with faith in You.

Lord, You have given me knowledge, wisdom, insight and revelation to see, hear, and understand. I declare in Jesus' name that I will know what it is that You have ordained for my children to do and be. You know their purpose. Anoint and grace me to discover, draw out, and deploy what You have already ordained for their lives.

As my child is being trained up in the way that they should go, let them love truth in their inward parts, and cause them to live by that truth. I declare that every spiritual gift, natural gift, and talent is consecrated to You--even their intellect--and they all shall be fruitful to Your liking, God.

Father, my offspring are seeds of Your Kingdom, The Kingdom of God. As a seed of purpose and destiny who lives intentionally, focused on their calling, grace them to impact their family, peers, coworkers, and all of the places that the soles of their feet tread for God's purposes.

I consecrate their inward man to You. Cause the influence of their Godly Spirit to rout the influences of their human nature. Grace them to live by the dictates of Holy Spirit and let them rejoice always in a life lived in the pursuit and the reality of righteousness. Let the mind of Christ dwell in them richly for His mind always led Him to do what was right; and from it the lives of people are always blessed. Let their mind be in perfect peace and let it continually be fixed on the Heavenly Father.

Whatever things have infiltrated the mind of my child with the potential of leading them astray--into wrong words, thoughts, and deeds--I declare the transforming and renewing of their mind so that it is renewed as relates to all of life. Lord, by Your spirit I release Your covering for protection over my child. I declare that every spirit and anointing for protection is activated now to guard and secure them. No weapon formed against my child shall prosper.

Daily I place them in Your care, God; and under the shadow of Your wings, Almighty One. As I place them in the cleft of the rock, let the security of their life be sealed by the Blood of Jesus, warring and ministering angels, and the anointing of Holy Spirit. I cry out to You, Lord, that nothing shall harm or injure them in Jesus' name. In You,

Lord, I declare them kept from all sickness, disease, infirmity, and any other thing that stands against the Kingdom of God.

Heavenly Father, I ask You to manifest prosperity, success and significance. I believe that these things are a part of Your preordained plan for my seed. I declare their life is dedicated and consecrated to You, and the fruit of increase and abundance is their portion in You, Jesus.

Finally, Father, turn my heart in a new way to my child's heart, and turn their heart to me in a new way. Let our hearts knit together as one, and by Your spirit, let them be knitted together forever. Lord, anoint my mothering and let my child benefit from Your work in me exceedingly, abundantly above all that I can ask and or think. I declare all of these things done and manifesting in the name of Jesus. Amen.

About the Author

Apostle Terrell Murphy brings more than 30 years of corporate, community and ministry experience to his role as Senior Pastor of Life Center International. Through his great love and compassion for the inner city of Charlotte in 2006

Apostle Murphy established City Dive, Inc., a 501(c)(3) organization designed to promote initiatives supporting its mission is to engage, equip and empower families to radically transform and sustain their lives and communities. He also serves as its current President and CEO.

Apostle Murphy is called as a reformer in the body of Christ. His compassion is to see the Kingdom order of God restored back to its original purpose in the earth. This, he believes, shall come to pass through the execution of New Testament Apostolic Ministry and Worship Centers.

To see the church aligned to the purposes and focuses of our Lord and His Christ is what will deliver the kingdoms of this world to our Lord."

Apostle Murphy is a native of Granite Falls, North Carolina and graduate of Appalachian State University where he received his Bachelors of Science Degree in Communications. He is a devoted husband to his wife Susan Murphy. Together they are the proud parents of two sons, Samuel and Johnathan.

Made in the USA
Las Vegas, NV
25 March 2023

69654741R00105